LOVE
IN RECOVERY

"As a woman who is currently traveling the road to recovery with sexual addiction, Rachael Killackey's words spoke directly to the wounded and tender places of my feminine heart. Her wisdom and compassion spring forth a well of hope in an area of struggle where so many women have felt unseen. With radical honesty, she takes the reader through a journey of intimacy with the Lord that goes far beyond sobriety and invites us to experience true healing."

Amanda
Magadala Ministries participant

"Killackey boldy dives into the various nuanced ways in which a woman's recovery from compulsive sexual behavior is unique and wonderful in its own rite, and she emerges victorious with several timeless dimensions of that process well explicated and grafted onto her own story of recovery for easier understanding. This thought-provoking read will prove helpful to many women in recovery and all those who care for them, for years to come"

Mary Jo Carney
Cofounder and associate director of formation
and campus partnerships
Magdala Ministries

"*Love in Recovery* is brilliantly written, theologically sound, and refreshinglyreal. Rachael Killackey's vulnerability in sharing her story offers hope to all who suffer in silence with pornography and sexual compulsion. I will recommend this book often!'"

Bob Schuchts
Author of *Be Healed*

"Killackey's book is an important contribution to a much-needed conversation in our Church about female sexual addiction. As a clinical psychologist who has walked with many young Catholic women struggling with compulsive sexual behaviors, I see in these pages the stories of so many who have felt invisible in our faith communities for far too long. Killackey's testimony is refreshingly honest and tender. She invites women struggling with compulsive sexual behaviors to move from suppression to surrender and from solitary confinement to refinement, and does so with wit and wisdom that are the fruit of her own deep psychological and spiritual exploration. Rather than offering a one-size-fits-all approach to recovery, Killackey offers an engaging account of her own journey of healing from addiction while seamlessly infusing practical wisdom along the way."

Julia Sadusky
Licensed clinical psychologist and owner of
Lux Counseling and Consulting

"I want to stand and cheer every time Killackey pulls back the curtain on another chapter of *Love in Recovery*. She speaks clearly about the impact of trauma, childhood exposure to pornography, and pain unique to each woman's experience, but she is undeterred in pointing toward hope, healing, and wholeness. With kindness and compassion, Killackey leads Catholic women on a restorative journey that brings them closer to Christ and his life-changing grace."

Sam Black
Author of *The Healing Church: What Churches Get Wrong
about Pornography and How to Fix It*

"*Love in Recovery* is a true gift to women seeking freedom from pornography addiction and lustful compulsions, blazing a trail of hope and healing on a topic that is too often directed toward men. Killackey's honest storytelling and guidance within this book will be lifesaving for many."

Scott Weeman
Founder of Catholic in Recovery

"The omnipresence of porn in our culture ensnares women, too. But our experiences—of shame, of woundedness, of healing—tend to go untold. Here is a book that finally breaks the silence. Adeptly weaving personal experience with theological reflection, historical analysis, and practical advice, Killackey brings a message of hope and freedom to her readers. We women are caught between the

Scylla and Charybdis of purity culture and porn culture; this brave and beautiful book illuminates a way out."

Abigail Favale
Author of *The Genesis of Gender: A Christian Theory*

"Women are often seen as the victims of pornography. What we often fail to discuss, however, is the fact that some women watch pornography of their own accord, and some of those women feel they simply cannot stop. Rachael Killackey is one such woman who was once hooked on pornography and is now bravely speaking out to other women who have fallen into the same trap. For the past ten or so years I've been speaking publicly on the topic of pornography and I've met countless teens, young women, and not-so-young women who've approached me and thanked me for not talking about pornography as if it's merely a guy's issue. I have been praying for the day when a woman (or an army of women) like Killackey would find the courage to share their own stories of addiction and recovery. This book is going to be a light and a balm to many. I'm so glad it exists."

Matt Fradd
Author of *The Porn Myth*

"Rachael Killackey is a fierce advocate and a safe heart for all those struggling with and suffering from the effects of pornography. Whether porn is a part of your past or your present, Rachael's authenticity, practical wisdom, and—above all—her compassion will shed healing light on your own story, as it did for me. I would recommend this book to anyone who has been wounded by pornography, which is to say, I recommend it to everyone."

Beth Davis
Director of Mission Advancement
Blessed is She

LOVE
IN RECOVERY

One Woman's Story of Breaking
Free from Shame and Healing from
Pornography Addiction

RACHAEL KILLACKEY

AVE MARIA PRESS AVE Notre Dame, Indiana

Nihil Obstat: Reverend Monsignor Michael Heintz, PhD
                  Censor Librorum

Imprimatur: Most Reverend Kevin C. Rhoades
                Bishop of Fort Wayne–South Bend
                Given at Fort Wayne, Indiana, on 18 November, 2022

The *Nihil Obstat* and *Imprimatur* are official declarations that a book or pamphlet is free of doctrinal or moral error. No implication is contained therein that those who have granted the *Nihil Obstat* or *Imprimatur* agree with its contents, opinions, or statements expressed.

Founded in 1865, Ave Maria Press is a ministry of the United States Province of Holy Cross.

www.avemariapress.com

Paperback: ISBN-13 978-1-64680-210-4

E-book: ISBN-13 978-1-64680-211-1

Cover image © Drypsiak / iStock / Getty Images Plus.

Cover and text design by Samantha Watson.

Printed and bound in the United States of America.

Library of Congress Cataloging-in-Publication Data is available.

The spirit has shifted, my body remains
In its old place. Pain overtakes me
To last as long as my body is growing.
Now I can give it food from the spirit
Where before there was only hunger.

At times love aches: there are weeks,
    months, years.
Like the roots of a dry tree, my tongue is
    dry
And the roof of my mouth. My lips are
    unpainted.
It takes long: Truth sounding out error.

But it is He who feels
The drought of the whole world, not I.

Magdalene, by St. John Paul II

CONTENTS

Introduction xi

Chapter 1: The Beginning 1

Chapter 2: The Problem with Purity Culture 21

Chapter 3: How We Got Here: The History of
      the Pornography Industry 35

Chapter 4: Waking Up 47

Chapter 5: Radical Honesty 65

Chapter 6: Recovering Relationship 79

Chapter 7: Wearing Your Face 95

Chapter 8: The Gateway Drugs 107

Chapter 9: The Practicals 121

Chapter 10: Restoring Imagination 135

Chapter 11: Recapturing Innocence 149

Chapter 12: The White Horse 161

Recommended Reading 169

Notes 171

INTRODUCTION

I will always remember very vividly the first time I publicly shared about my struggle with pornography. I was in the mountains of North Carolina at a Young Life camp, leading a group of more than a dozen high schoolers through a week of encountering Jesus. One of the activities of the week was called a "cardboard testimony," in which leaders wrote on one side of a piece of cardboard a struggle or sin they'd had in their lives and, on the flip side, how Jesus had redeemed them.

In a meeting with all the Young Life leaders, the camp directors told us about these testimonies and asked us to be bold and vulnerable. We had to write down what we would put on our cardboard and submit it to the camp directors, and they would select a handful of people to present in front of the crowd. I immediately thought of my struggle with pornography, and I quickly wrote it down before I could change my mind. I told the Lord that if he wanted me to, I would share.

The next day, when the camp directors read off the names of whom they'd selected, my name was first on the list.

At the end of the camp week, the time for presenting the testimonies came. I was scared to death. I had knots in my stomach and felt like puking, but on one side of that piece of cardboard I wrote "Chained by an addiction to pornography" and, on the other half, "Set free by Christ's pure love." I remember coming out on stage holding my cardboard between my hands and feeling the knots in my stomach slowly disappear. Afterward, freeing tears fell as I spoke with other students and leaders. I'll never forget one of the camp directors who came up to me, took my hand, and said, "God bless you. If only you could know what you've done—a woman saying this is so rare. God bless you."

I had just finished my sophomore year of college, and I was almost a year clean then. It seems I haven't been able to shut up about pornography addiction since. What started as something I felt convicted to share once, maybe twice, has become the dearest mission to my heart. Five years after that cardboard testimony, I founded an organization that helps women recover from addictions to pornography, masturbation, and other sexual sins through small groups and other resources. That mission is one of the deepest wells of joy present in my life.

I couldn't seem to shut up about women's struggle with sexual sin because I felt that no one was talking about it. While I quickly found I was far from the only one with the call to address the topic placed on my heart, I believe there's only a need for more. As secularism and the pornography industry continue increasing their audiences, we have to continue to increase ours. I needed this message as a young teenager, as a young woman—and I know now that I'm not the only one. The death grip that addiction has on our culture will only increase if we stay silent; however terrifying sharing our personal stories may be—whether it's on a piece of cardboard in front of four hundred people or in a conversation with a friend—it's the only way to loosen that grip.

Here you'll find the story of my own struggle with pornography—largely kept secret and hidden from those around me for several years—my recovery journey, and the healing of deep shame that caused my struggle with pornography to begin with. I am not a licensed therapist, and this book is not a substitute for receiving clinical help. If you are battling an addiction to pornography or any other harmful substance or behavior, please seek help from a trustworthy clinician. However, in this book, I give you what I do have—the complexity of one woman's story and the hope of healing that can be found only in Jesus Christ. Not only did his love pursue me in this dark place, but also I have seen him reach into the stories of hundreds of men and women and offer redemption they never thought was possible.

So often, freedom begins simply in hearing a story that sounds like ours. Isolation feeds addictions; communion starves them. I desperately needed a woman to share her story when I was a teenager and young adult—a story that sounded like the one I kept silent for too long. In this book, I'm offering you a story, whether or not you need it as I did.

Thank you for receiving my story. I pray it's a benefit to you in your journey toward heaven, whether or not you are a woman who struggles with sexual sin. This book will act somewhat as my "cardboard testimony" did: I'll flip between the sin itself—how it felt and kept me coming back—and the healing work of Christ. As you read, I encourage you to invite the Holy Spirit to take you beneath the surface of your own story and reveal the place where woundedness and shame seem to have the final word. Pornography, masturbation, and other sexual sins are symptoms of a deeper problem; healing isn't about simply becoming sober. It's about encountering, perhaps for the first time, the intimacy we long for with God, others, and ourselves.

Finally, if this book stirs something in you, *reach out to someone*. Whether you've kept your sin and struggle hidden, know of a friend who needs more support, or just want to start a larger conversation about sexual sin and shame, don't let the message stop with you. Healing happens communally, not in isolation. Your story could be *the* story someone else needs. One of the phrases my team and I turn to consistently in our apostolate is "redeemed sexuality"—I believe it's possible for you, for me, for anyone who reaches out their hand to Christ's eternally outstretched one. If you need a beacon of hope that it *is* possible, I pray this book is it and that no matter what you've done, you'll reach out your hand.

1
THE BEGINNING

There is no need to be dismayed if love sometimes follows torturous ways. Grace has the power to make straight the paths of human love.

–Pope John Paul II

Where to Begin

Over a year ago at a nearby parish, I was giving a Theology on Tap talk to a small, co-ed audience. My topic was Healing from Pornography Addiction. One woman walked in a few minutes late; quietly taking a seat next to her friend in the front row, I overheard her whisper, "What is this talk about again?"

"Porn addiction," her friend replied.

The first woman looked at me and then whispered back, "But she's a *girl*."

I wasn't at all offended by her overheard comment; in fact, it's kind of the name of the game when it comes to the work I do now. Often I have to support—with believable statistics (I'll bore you with a few later)—the fact that I'm a part of an apostolate helping women heal from addictions to pornography, masturbation, and other sexual compulsions. The talks I give or podcast episodes I am featured in have to bear titles like "Women Struggle with

Pornography, Too" and "Women and Sexual Addiction." That's not a problem, but I hope one day it's different and the conversation about women struggling with sexual sin and compulsion is a norm, whether stats are cited or not.

This isn't a self-help book, because I don't think I could write one even if I wanted to. What I can write is a story and one woman's musings on recovery and the human heart. Talking about sexual sin in the Church often involves a primarily practical conversation, with the spiritual and psychological taking a back seat. While there are many helpful practicals out there—and we'll cover some of them, don't worry—talking about sexual addiction and sin for women can't start there.

St. Thomas Aquinas's *Summa Theologiae* revolves around a striking theme referred to as *exitus-reditus,* or the principle that all created things come from God (*exitus*) and are ordered toward returning to him (*reditus*). God's love is what we were created out of and what we're ultimately drawn toward returning to—and we were given free will to choose. Sexuality isn't excluded from what God created, and it's ordered by the same principle. It's not a place that God ignores in humans but a place he *invites* us. So much of healing from any sin, sexual sin included, involves a recognition of precisely this—that our sexuality comes from God and can return to him.

In his brilliant and pivotal papal audiences that were ultimately compiled into his Theology of the Body, Pope John Paul II beautifully illustrates how Christ "appeals to the beginning" through human sexuality—Christ reminds us where we've come from, and our origin reveals our intended end. In order to explore the falls of human sexuality—female sexuality, in this case—one has to begin with what the *purpose* of it is; the unique gifts and beauty of the feminine heart and body set the tone for the very way the enemy wants to tempt us. Only in knowing the purpose of our sexuality can we find the reason and origins of our brokenness, as well as the healing that reminds us whom we're on a journey of returning to.

Through my work and my own story, I've become intimate with the brokenness of sexual sin. As you'll read in these pages, my grappling with the reality of pornography and the damage it inflicted on my body and soul was one of the greatest battles of my life to date. But, by the grace of God, because of this brokenness, I've also been able to become intimate with the hope and healing only he can provide. We all live our own journey of being broken and receiving his personal "appeal to the beginning"—the call to remember where we've come from and where our Home truly is. Our brokenness can be either the source of our despair or an opportunity to see the intentionality, love, and dignity with which we were made. It's an invitation to die to the old man and embrace the new one, in the language of St. Paul. My work is now dedicated precisely to helping women receive this invitation in their sexuality, and I've been given the gift of encountering the stories of hundreds of them at all stages of their journeys. The conversation, and subsequently this book, isn't truly about pornography, masturbation, lust, or sexual sin in general but rather about the eternal beckoning of a God who radically loves us. I know for a fact that if I hadn't experienced the fallenness of sexual sin, I would not know the love of Jesus as I do now. The Church, every year at Easter Vigil, praises God for this paradox of love: "O happy fault, O necessary sin of Adam, which gained for us so great a Redeemer!"[1]

On a macrocosmic scale, the Garden must be discussed before the Fall, and so it is with the microcosmic when discussing our own lives. Our origin must be understood before our downfall truly can be. I want to begin with the beauty and intentionality of the feminine mind, soul, and body, and invite you—particularly if you're a woman—to hear Christ's appeal to *your* beginning. Your sexuality is intricate and stunningly complex. Your woundedness and sinfulness—and mine—cannot make sense without first understanding this.

Sadly, a lot of what's behind the misconception about women struggling with sexual addiction comes not from just a disbelief about women grappling with sin in their sexuality but from an ignorance of women's sexuality in general. From our social conversations to school education and even a majority of our conversations in church, we lack the understanding of God's design for women and that our sexuality is a massive part of honoring that design. Part of why different iterations of the phrase "women have sexual struggles, too!" need to be used so often is because we don't often think of women as sexual beings *in the first place*. Not only *are* we sexual beings, but also our sexuality is a fundamental part of God's plan for our holiness and for the way we give his life to the world.

God's Plan for Woman

Since she was the final creation of God in Genesis, *woman* is often referred to as the "crown jewel of creation," which is a pretty stunning title—unless it's being used toward you in a sorry attempt at a Catholic pickup line. In all seriousness, this term truly does reflect the intentionality of God when creating woman, when we examine it closely. When we read the creation narrative in Genesis, there's a *buildup* to the creation of woman in the person of Eve; Adam's exclamation at the sight of her is one of both awe and fulfillment:

> This one, at last, is bone of my bones
> and flesh of my flesh;
> This one shall be called "woman,"
> for out of man this one has been taken. (Gn 2:23)

Recognizing his inherent similarity to Eve in their mutual personhood—since she was fashioned literally from his own rib—Adam also gives her a unique name, and he sees how she differs from him. Their differences aren't for the sake of division—though, in a state of sin, they certainly become such—but rather for their ultimate complementarity in God's design. Put simply, there is something about man alone that isn't complete, just as woman alone is not complete; as God says earlier on in Genesis, "It is not good for the man to be alone" (Gn 2:18). When God expresses his intention to make human beings in his image, he's expressing that the image is only completed once woman is in the picture.

This is where the title "crown jewel of creation" comes from. It's signifying that woman is the final brushstroke of the true Artist, the Author of all creation. It doesn't make women better or more dignified, but it does mean we're fashioned with an intentionality to carry a beauty that *only we can*. The beauty and complementarity that struck awe in Adam are still there in every woman, whatever her relationship with men might be or however she feels about herself. Even if they're buried beneath a surface of sin and regret, they're still there. There is still something incomplete about God's creation without her living fully.

As Anglican author William Gurnall says, "It is this image of God reflected in you that so enrages hell; it is this at which the demons hurl their mightiest weapons."[2] If fully living out beauty and the intentionality of God's design is how we best imagine him, you'd better believe that it's exactly what the enemy will set his sights on destroying. I'm not talking about physical beauty, though that's certainly inherent to every woman, whether or not she or others believe it. I'm talking about the beauty that pierces us, wounds us, and leaves us open and exposed for the intimate work of God. It's *his* beauty, not ours—but he tasked us with being unique vessels of it. Adam's very exclamation at the sight of Eve is enough to confirm that her beauty was astounding—even more so because at the time, she was untainted by sin and thus a pure reflection of the image of God.

Pope Benedict XVI says, "The encounter with the beautiful can become the wound of the arrow which strikes the heart, and in this way opens our eyes."[3] Female beauty, when ordered toward and surrendered to our Creator, can become a small arrow that pierces the hearts of those around us, leaving them hungry for the true beauty of God. This is why we're the target of the enemy—he knows all too well what beauty can do in the hands of its Maker and what it can do when we take it into our own hands.

A woman's beauty and uniqueness lie chiefly in the fact that she gives life to *more* beauty, whether by biologically sustaining and giving life through children or by fostering and nurturing life spiritually in those around her. The philosopher and theologian Alice von Hildebrand attributes the enemy's attacks on women to this particular beautiful gift: "Since Genesis, the one deadly enemy of the serpent is the woman because she has been named 'mother of the living.' This is confirmed by God Himself. Therefore the enemy's most vicious attacks will be directed against her."[4] Since "the glory of God is man fully alive," as St. Irenaeus said, the enemy simply *does not want humanity to live*. The life-giving beauty of women—again, in both physical and spiritual senses—becomes his target so that he can cut off life, and therefore the glory of God, at its source.

If you're reading this and you're a woman, this isn't some far-off theological musing of dead guys. This is *you*. It doesn't matter whether you're young, married, a mother, in religious life, or wondering what the heck to do with your life—you have been tasked with beauty and the begetting of human life. Maybe this call is manifested through giving birth to and raising children; maybe it's through your relationships, community, service, or workplace. Whatever the case, you *are* a vessel of beauty and meant to pierce the heart of humanity, creating a longing to be fully alive. Your feminine sexuality is the outward expression of this call. Our sexuality isn't limited to sexual *behavior*; it's the way we interact physically with the world. I interact with the world, others, and God as a human being *who is a woman*. I cannot get around my feminine sexuality or ignore it; instead, I have to participate with it in order to find God's call for my life—his call for me *as a woman*.

The drama of God's intentionality in creating us, as well as the intensity of the enemy's attacks against us, also isn't fictional. It's playing out in your life, whether obviously or not. Our ordering and call are lofty, so that means our woundedness is deep. I am convinced the enemy has been unleashing a blatant, horrific, and twisted attack against women in our modern age precisely through feminine sexuality. As the twentieth-century philosopher Edith Stein notes in a haunting summary, "Because the sin she caused [Adam] to commit was in all likelihood a sin of sensuality, woman is more intensely exposed to the danger of descent into stark carnality. And when this happens, she always becomes once again the evil seductress, whereas, paradoxically, God has specifically enjoined her to combat evil."[5] Her analysis is beyond accurate. A woman's beauty—*your* beauty—is either a vessel for the life that can only come from God or a tool for humanity's destruction. The Russian novelist Fyodor Dostoyevsky once said, "Beauty is mysterious as well as terrible. God and devil are fighting there, and the battlefield is the heart of man."[6] This isn't meant to frighten us as women or make us scrupulous about every move we make or our appearance; it's meant to be a convicting call to return to God's original purpose for our nature and recognize the plan of the enemy in trying to subvert it.

Feminine sexuality is incredibly, breathtakingly beautiful—with the potential to be so noble and awe-inspiring that, to borrow from Dostoyevsky, it's a worthy battleground on which God and Satan wage war. This happens on a cultural level and on a personal level for each woman who came after Eve. Throughout these pages, we'll explore reasons why pornography and other sexual sins became more and more tempting for women in our modern age and what their specific effects on feminine sexuality are. But for now, it's most important to understand that God has the intention to bring humanity *to him* through the beauty of our sexuality, and the enemy has the intention to wound you and others through it so that beauty cannot accomplish its purpose. Remember: since our sexuality, our *being a woman*, is a place where we carry the image of God, hell spares no expense in attacking it.

As Catholics, we have such a unique gift in our Church's honoring of the Blessed Mother. In her we find the original intention for the beauty of woman in creation, so much so that her entire self, including her feminine sexuality, was *completely surrendered* to God and brought him physically into the world in her son. All of us have been fooled by the temptations of our enemy to use our one beautiful feminine life for things other than, or even completely opposed to, God. In Mary, we can look to what God designed us to be and ask her to accompany us on our way to being more like her. In moments where it's been easy for me to feel discouraged about ever having a close relationship with Mary because of such deep imperfection, particularly in my sexuality, it's been comforting to remember that both she *and* St. Mary Magdalene, the patroness of the ministry I'm currently a part of, were present at the Crucifixion of our Lord. There's something deeply restorative about that: the sinless woman and the woman who had seven demons cast out of her united at the foot of the Cross. The only thing Mary wants is to bring us closer to her son. She doesn't compare, compete, or condemn, and she's the surest guide as we journey toward overcoming and healing from our sin. When we forget what we are able to become with God's grace, she's there to remind us.

No woman since has met the ideal that Mary did. All of our expressions of our sexuality have been inhibited by our own woundedness and sin. Despite the fact that none of us will ever embody this perfectly as Mary did, the call remains the same. It's the appeal to the beginning that Christ gives to every female heart—to strive to surrender ourselves entirely to him and to live out our call to foster, defend, and exemplify the Christian call to nurture life, receive the grace of God, and allow his beauty to wound us. We carry this call both in soul and body, and it's where our sexuality finds its significance and sanctification—and where our woundedness and sin find us.

Defining Feminine Sexual Woundedness

The therapist and minister Jay Stringer, in his incredible work on sexual brokenness *Unwanted*, says that our sexual brokenness is "the geography of God's arrival."[7] For a long time, I took what I would call a "white-knuckle" approach to sexual sin and imperfection—something we'll discuss heavily in this book. Instead of allowing the call God has placed on my feminine heart to be a lens at through I looked at my own brokenness and allowed myself to be invited back to his plan when I strayed, I saw my brokenness simply as invitations to be discouraged. This had more to do with what I thought of God than what I thought of myself. Stringer's question asks us to, in a way, reorient not just the way we see our sin but also the way we think *God* sees our sin. He doesn't enjoy our brokenness or take any delight in it, nor in our sin, but he *does* delight in healing and rescuing us from it all, just as Stringer points out. Continually he invites us to return to who he created us to be—to shed the old woman and live as the new, time and time again.

Woundedness, including sexual woundedness, is part of every person's life. Some may read that sentence and think it's not true because they've never been victims of sexual abuse, but that's an *incredibly* limited definition of woundedness. Sexual woundedness can come in many forms: Dr. Bob Schuchts, in his book *Be Restored*, cites several categories of sexual and psychosexual violations that most people will easily identify with and that result in wounding whether we identify it or not. The sexual violations include *forceful sexual abuse, seductive sexual abuse, sexual sin,* and *sexual play,* while the psychosexual violations include *attachment wounds, gender confusion, isolation, peer rejection, disordered desires,* and more.[8] Even a *lack* of proper sexual education and being left to find things out on your own can be a form of sexual wounding. Every human heart past the age of reason—no matter how sheltered, virtuous, or mature—can look at Schucht's list and find at least one category where a violation has happened, even if it was self-inflicted, as with sexual sin. Wherever the violation occurs and no matter who the perpetrator is (or what they intended), it results in a wound because it was an action against our dignity as men and women made in the image and likeness of God.

One woman once articulated her pain over engaging in sexual play as a child—something that, at first glance, may not seem like a big deal and rather just something we'd like to chock up to another embarrassing moment in our childhood. "It made me feel like I was . . . made wrong," she said. "It made me feel like all I can create is dirt and sin." The tears in her eyes, recounting even all these years later, told me how deep that pain went and the wound that came with it. In her simple and honest words we can clearly see the wound to her call to carry beauty. The enemy tells her through those events in her childhood that she can't *possibly* be beautiful in body and soul because of what she did, and her memories make it easy for her to believe him.

Within ministry I've seen firsthand the many forms sexual woundedness takes. Women have recounted to me their moments of experimenting sexually with their first boyfriends, curiously exploring their bodies as children, or what has felt like their lifelong lack of control over their own thoughts. Still more cry from the pain of tense, difficult, or nonexistent relationships with either or both of their parents, bullying from classmates, or even heartbreaking experiences of being victims of sexual violence. Whatever the level of gravity of those heavy experiences, almost all of them say something similar to the women above: they feel as if they were *made wrong*, that all they're capable of is creating gross, horrible, sinful things and that their call to be beautiful is permanently damaged or revoked. Almost all of them feel alienated in one way or another from God's plan for femininity—that other women may be capable of fulfilling it but that they're prevented. It's a feeling I recognize all too well.

Wounds Prepare Us for Exposure

The beginning of sexual confusion and woundedness in my life came first in my childhood from a few instances that violated sexual boundaries by people outside my family. While I may never know the intention of the men and boys in question, I do know how their actions made me feel: strange, ashamed, awkward, and incredibly confused. I carried this confusion and awkwardness with me throughout my childhood, and accompanying the confusion was a high level of curiosity about physicality and sexuality. With what I know now, I'm able to see that my curiosity was me simply trying to seek answers for the things that had made me feel violated and confused, as is the case with many of us. Subconsciously, part of me believed that if I were able to understand sexuality and sex, I would be able to possess a certain control over it, thereby silencing the confusion, discomfort, and feelings of powerlessness within me.

Looking at my experiences through the lens of Christ's invitation to women—what my heart and body were created for—I can see the wounds articulate something much deeper and more excruciating than just awkwardness or confusion. Something in me felt that I was *meant* to feel awkward, that I invited or was destined for uncomfortable experiences—this was my version of believing I was somehow "created wrong." My experiences led me to believe that my feminine beauty *invited* violation or awkwardness, or that it was only ever going to be dangerous or uncomfortable to live out. As I got older, I envied the comfort other girls seemed to have with themselves; for my part, though I have a fairly bold and confident personality, I felt strange and out of place in my developing femininity. I felt at many moments as if I didn't fit in with other girls, yet I felt awkward in the presence of men. These feelings of isolation and awkwardness felt deep-seated and integral to me; they felt like part of my body, my *identity*.

When encountering our woundedness, we often reach for one of two extremes—allowing it to define us or disregarding it completely. We can do this without even recognizing it. However, the inconvenient thing about wounds is that they will continue to rage and express themselves through our thoughts and actions *until* we acknowledge them and allow them to be healed. I wrote off these experiences in my childhood for a long, long time, thinking they weren't grave enough and didn't actually matter. It wasn't until I opened them up in my adulthood and saw them for what they were—moments of wounding—that the discomfort I thought I would carry for the rest of my life started to disappear. In the meantime, I would look elsewhere for a solution to it; we are all looking for answers to the questions left by our wounds and experiences. As a confused, uncomfortable, and curious young girl, I was primed and ready for pornography to pose itself as my answer.

Exposure

I remember the day of my first exposure quite vividly. It was day, though I can't remember what time, but I remember how sunny my room was. I was on my bed, scrolling through Pinterest on a family laptop used for our homeschooling. I was thirteen and about to begin eighth grade. As I scrolled, I came across a short fanfiction piece about a band I liked. I read it, and then read another, and then came across one that was graphically sexual about a particular band member. To say it was intriguing is an understatement; it grabbed at my already-existent curiosity about sexuality, beckoning it to find the control it so desperately wanted through a disordered knowledge. I justified reading that first piece of written porn by telling myself I knew the things they were doing were wrong and that I wouldn't do them.

My young conscience also felt so hesitant and afraid as I read, begging me to stop, telling me I knew better. Of course I did, and I knew better than to keep reading—but I was hooked, and one story led to another. After closing the laptop that day and the mindless binge was over, I didn't suddenly feel "in control." The interior confusion that I had carried for years only deepened. Eventually I was able to admit in my young mind that what I had read was pornography, but I believed it was a "less extreme" version than the images or videos that I originally thought pornography was limited to. I tried to shove it under the rug and mentally committed to never reading any of it again. Unfortunately, as many social media platforms do, Pinterest had an algorithm that would display content similar to what I had previously viewed on my home feed. As is probably obvious, since this is a book about pornography addiction, the first time for me wasn't the last time.

The relationship between woundedness and sin is a strange one. People wonder why they pursue the very things that only seem to drive the knife into the places where they're already hurting; I've seen this over and over in my own journey and in my work now. Why is it that I was so attracted to porn when the very feelings of confusion and shame that I was trying to rid myself of were just fed by it? Put simply, pornography fit perfectly into the framework of sexuality that I was already operating in as a young girl. The feeling of shame as I closed the laptop after my first reading binge wasn't new; it was a familiar place for me, already set up by my unwanted experiences. Because we're broken, we have a strange way of making a home in the lies we're sold through our wounds. Porn was a new way for me to hear the same lies I had already been hearing: that I was meant for awkwardness, confusion, discomfort, ugliness, *sin*—that my very being invited it.

If I did confess to reading porn in Confession after those first times, I did it in such a vague way that I can't even remember if I did. I wouldn't name it "pornography" in the confessional until much later; instead, I would use phrases like "I watched something harmful to my purity" or "I had an objectifying thought about someone." Abundantly clear, right? I was scared to death of what it could mean to admit this to myself and what a priest might think.

From there, an exposure while innocently scrolling through Pinterest turned into a five-year battle with pornography that quickly moved beyond reading graphic fanfiction. I was hesitant, as are many other women I've encountered, to say that I was an addict, solely because I didn't use porn sites to find the porn I was watching. This is where mindsets perhaps have to be confronted—pornography, by definition, is "the depiction of erotic behavior (as in pictures or writing) intended to cause sexual excitement."[9] By definition, it is not limited to solely visual content or to sites that are designed to host that content. If we operate by this definition, pornography can be found easily on YouTube and in TV shows, movies, and books, and we have the ability to create it in our own minds—a topic that I will address later on in this book. I found pornography on platforms accessed by millions of people on a daily basis, including children, but explicit sexual content is there in abundance. "Age restrictions" on these sites are often just essentially a dressed-up warning or slap on the wrist, and they are all too easy to bypass.

Defining Addiction

I don't specifically remember how frequently I accessed pornography, and despite what some may think, that's not uncommon. It's important here to recognize that clinicians define addiction not by the frequency of use (though frequency can definitely be an alarm bell that an addiction is present) but rather by criteria that help evaluate whether a certain behavior is inhibiting your free will and livelihood. Gerald May, a psychiatrist who wrote a groundbreaking book for Christians on addiction titled *Addiction and Grace*, defines addiction as "any compulsive, habitual behavior that limits the freedom of human desire."[10] He also lays out the following criteria to assess the presence of an addiction: *tolerance, loss of willpower, withdrawal symptoms, self-deception*, and *distortion of attention*.[11] Tolerance means that your resistance to the substance or behavior builds, and you therefore need more of it in order to achieve the desired result. Loss of willpower points to the desire of the addict to stop using the substance or doing the behavior, but the addict is unable to quit based on their own willpower. Withdrawal symptoms indicate that a whole host of adverse effects occur when the addict doesn't engage in the substance or behavior: these can be physical and mental, such as fatigue or anxiety. Self-deception, which May notes is one of the "most significant hallmarks" of addiction, is the ability of the addict to invent reasons for using the substance or engaging in the behavior. Conflicting desires, mixed emotions, and an interior back-and-forth ensue; think of the old devil on one shoulder, angel on the other that's comically depicted in many movies. Finally, distortion of attention is the lack of self-control that the addict experiences; when they are triggered to use or engage in a behavior, they are unable to resist the thought or temptation. When it arises, it diverts their attention from anything else—family, work, God—and results ultimately in a perpetual preoccupation with the substance or behavior. The mind easily jumps to thinking about it, and it's almost impossible to refocus its attention on the present moment when it does.

The above criteria are helpful to know, and I recommend keeping them in mind. Often people ask me how to "know" if they or a loved one is addicted, and I point to this list. True addiction, which May says we *all* experience in minor or major ways, is instead indicated by the presence of the above criteria, making addiction a lot more common than we'd like to think. If there's a behavior or substance that's exercising any sort of control over you, whether by dictating how you use your time, causing you to lie to yourself and others, negatively influencing your thoughts, or causing you to seek it out in moments of pain, stress, sadness, or other emotional discomfort, there's the potential for addiction, if it isn't an addiction already.

I certainly saw the presence of the criteria in my own life, but it took several years for me to actually admit it. Part of that was me just being young and having very little context for my struggle—but part of it was also my increasing ability to reason with the addiction and keep it around. "Others do it more than I do," "I can stop whenever I want," and "It hasn't been bad this month" were all phrases my mind was quite familiar with by the end of high school. But fanfiction escalated to videos, and my attention was easily diverted by fantasizing with images and lustful thoughts and a desire to act out by consuming more content. For me, "acting out" almost never included masturbation, which women struggle with in an even higher percentage than pornography. The "high" I experienced solely from consuming pornography was enough; it temporarily alleviated the awkwardness and confusion I felt in my sexuality, though it left me only feeling it more potently afterward.

Since beginning to speak publicly on the topic of sexual addiction in women and healing sexual sin in general, one of the weirdest reactions I've gotten—sadly, more than once—has been from others who have attempted to write my story off. This happened to a lot of women I've walked with as well, and it seriously gets my goat. I'll discuss this more in the next chapter, but I can't tell you how harmful it is to make addiction a competition, not to mention how strange it is to want to have a monopoly on porn addiction specifically by trying to gauge how deeply entrenched someone else is. I'm incredibly grateful that I was protected from a *lot* of different types of porn by not accessing specific porn sites, but to evaluate someone's struggle based on where and what they are consuming is completely missing the point. We should never make each other "prove" how bad our sin and addiction are or was; in a way, that's giving glory to evil by making it some sort of qualification or badge the more evil it becomes. This is also why having solid criteria like Gerald May's above is so important when we're discussing addiction. It's not only about the gravity of the content itself—first and foremost, it's about the *control* that content has over your life.

I also think the details of my exposure to and accessing of pornography at a fairly young age are important, not just for the sake of this book but also because I find that many parents downplay the possibility of their children being exposed to pornography. I received a Catholic education and was homeschooled for several years in a large (by cultural standards), devout Catholic family. I've journeyed with many women who are from similar backgrounds and still wound up addicted to sexual compulsions. My parents instilled in me a love for God early in my life and a desire to prioritize prayer and the pursuit of virtue. They were careful about the media that we were allowed to consume as a family, and they instilled a firm but compassionate moral code in me and my siblings. Many psychologists are beginning to say that it's not about *if* your child is exposed to pornography but *when*—and I'd die on that hill. This isn't meant to be a threat but rather a warning to prepare us: if parenthood is part of our vocation, we have to be ready to keep a close eye on the media consumption of our current or future children and make sure that conversations about pornography, masturbation, and other sexual sins are both clear and compassionate. The expectation that just because you come from a devout family means you aren't at risk for addiction to pornography and masturbation is limited and idealistic when presented with factual data, and it only results in more shame and children going into deeper hiding when they *are* exposed. Sin and addiction thrive in darkness, so it's crucial that families—regardless of devotion, piety, moral rigor, or technological limitations—are willing to bring these topics to light.

It is also worth noting that while thirteen is young, the average age of exposure to pornography is even younger. Many resources once cited eleven as the average age of a child who is exposed to pornography for the first time, though a more recent study changed that number to the age of nine.[12] I've spoken with men and women who were as young as four or five years old at the time of their first exposure. Again, while this statistic is heartbreaking, it's not meant to scare parents into hypervigilance. Instead, we have to prepare children to encounter the world and the evil in it; the home is the place where they learn to either hide their sin or bring it to the merciful arms of the Father. If, as a Church, we continue to cultivate parishes, schools, and home environments that speak about sexuality, pornography, masturbation, and other sins in a way that's both convicted and compassionate and *welcomes mistakes*, perhaps addictions will not hide in the shadows for so long.

My parents instilled in me a knowledge that pornography was wrong to consume, and they truly did their best with the resources and knowledge they had. Our conversations about it, however, were not necessarily thorough—and I assumed that they, too, thought pornography was only a men's issue. Because of this, I didn't think it was acceptable for me to go to them as a girl struggling with pornography, and so it stayed hidden for many years. I recall telling a male friend briefly early on in high school, but I said nothing about it being an ongoing problem. I only mentioned my first exposure to him, trying to comfort him and relate as he disclosed his own struggles with sexual sin. It remained my secret until late high school.

I told my dearest friend, Clare, first; I believe it was in the midst of a conversation about a guy in high school that I was questioning if I had feelings for. I felt deeply unworthy of him—a feeling that would arise again and again in the presence of good men—and my friend prodded at why. I told her about my struggle in full, and her response was only merciful and good. I don't remember the moment particularly well, but I do remember that her reaction made it safe for me to share my story again later. I am very fortunate that my first conversation about my addiction was well received. As I said earlier, cultivating an environment where young teens especially are encouraged to bring sexual sin to light and abandon themselves to the mercy of God is no small feat. However, if that environment is *not* created or someone receives a negative reaction from a loved one or trusted figure in their life when they disclose their suffering, what results is a deep shame that can perpetuate an addiction for *years*. Without that openness to imperfect sexuality (which we all have) and the encouragement to bring it to God, any conversation about mercy and repentance becomes twisted: "It's safe to bring other things to God, but not *this*. He can't forgive you." I believed somewhere, because of the lack of context I had for women struggling with pornography, that maybe God didn't have a context for it either. As long as my addiction went on, I felt more and more like an anomaly, and the messaging around me only pushed me further to the outskirts.

It would take years of work both to overcome my addiction and the crippling shame that accompanied it and to dispel the confusion and discomfort about sexuality that had come as a result of my wounds. The work began by accepting that *my wounds weren't my fault*. When I think of the mindsets I had about God's mercy and myself then and the ones I have now, I praise God for the change and the freedom he's provided. Recovery from pornography is never just about stopping sinful habits and breaking addictive cycles; it's about allowing the grace of God to transform those mindsets that kept us trapped in the first place. Ultimately, it's about receiving the invitation to experience his love in the places where our wounds and needs are crying out through our sin, instead of trying to grit our teeth and somehow get the sinful habits out of our lives on our own.

Even more deeply than the mindsets instilled in me through my family and community were those I adopted from an unhealthy reality often linked with the chastity movement—a reality now called "purity culture." If I could say one thing is responsible particularly for the silence of women who are addicted to pornography and masturbation, I would say it's this. Exploring what was true and false in this messaging was necessary for my own healing, and I believe it is necessary for the healing of many others. What was and still is true in most chastity talks is the discussion about the inherent beauty and dignity of women. But as we're about to explore, what wasn't often articulated was that the invitation of Christ to return "to the beginning" remains, no matter how far we fall.

I've seen strides made—even since that Theology on Tap talk not too long ago—toward women's needs and sexual struggles being acknowledged and spoken about with compassion, love, and conviction. I genuinely hope that one day, people won't react to me or another woman speaking about the topics of sexual sin and addiction by saying, "But she's a *girl*," even though I understand why they do. What needs to change first, though, is a return to authentic conversations about the virtue of chastity without the influence of purity culture.

2
THE PROBLEM WITH PURITY CULTURE

The body, and it alone, is capable of making visible what is invisible: the spiritual and the divine. It was created to transfer into the visible reality of the world the mystery hidden since time immemorial in God [God's love for man], and thus to be a sign of it.
–Pope St. John Paul II, *Man and Woman He Created Them: A Theology of the Body*

Chastity versus "Purity Culture"

With the dawn of the sexual revolution—or what my moral theology teacher in high school called "the dark days of the '60s and '70s," with an unmistakably foreboding tone—the Church had a great deal of mess to wade through. Many books touch on the corruption of the definition of human freedom, but that corruption became most obvious in the pervasion of human sexuality. In the face of a rapidly disintegrating sexual ethic, the Church had a choice: to let the train keep heading south, *really* fast, or to crack down.

A bulk of that "cracking down" was, and is, incredibly beautiful. Out of the mess of the sexual revolution came works like Pope St. John Paul II's *Theology of the Body* and conversations about sexuality that finally gave it the dignity it deserved. In an effort to communicate the truths the Church was unearthing and dusting off, many clergy and laypeople alike began to spread the message of chastity, especially to teens and young adults. The *Catechism of the Catholic Church* defines chastity as "the successful integration of sexuality within the person and thus the inner unity of man in his bodily and spiritual being"(*CCC* 2337). It's the virtue one obtains when the outward expression of their body is in line with the dignity of their soul and is in accordance with their state in life. St. Thomas Aquinas notes, almost humorously, that chastity derives its name from the fact that "reason 'chastises' concupiscence which, like a child, needs curbing."[1] Again, we see that chastity is the virtue by which we physically see grace and reason correct the course of concupiscence or the human tendency to sin.

This being said, the message of chastity was and is abundantly necessary. I've seen it portrayed incredibly well, and I've seen it take a wrong turn, thus creating purity culture. Instead of encouraging virtue, it instills fear and performance-based standards, such as "Your body is like a perfectly wrapped present, and every time you give yourself away to someone, even in little ways, a bit of your wrapping is torn off," or "If someone hands you gum that's already been chewed, do you want to chew it? That's what marrying someone who hasn't been pure is like!" Pretty different from the motivating, all-encompassing virtue of chastity, right? It's important to distinguish the two because the need to practice chastity as a Christian—in any state in life—never ends. However, in the long run, purity culture, while it may be well intentioned, only ends up harming the pursuit of the virtue of chastity.

Purity culture began largely in evangelical Christian churches, where upright and moral people were also trying to respond to the damage of the sexual revolution, but *without* the help of brilliant, balanced minds like Pope St. John Paul II. It took the embodied virtue of chastity and the truth of that message and collapsed it into a list of "dos and don'ts," fear tactics, generalizations, and heaps of shame. It largely used scripture to support its claims, though several books written in the past decade have exhibited how unfounded in scripture many of those claims are.

Purity culture didn't limit itself solely to evangelical Christianity but found its way into Catholicism as well. Many Catholics spreading the message of chastity adopted certain tactics or generalizations regularly found in purity culture, in an effort to preserve young people from the pain of sexual sin. It's a mistake to throw the baby out with the bathwater and dismiss the pursuit of chastity or the content of these Catholics solely because of certain disagreeable content they may have presented in the past. However, I do find that many women, including myself, have to take some time to sort through and heal from those missteps, and I believe that can be done in a way that still receives the truth and supports these people in their intended mission.

Purity Culture and Pornography

One of the greatest and I believe most harmful elements of purity culture is to make sweeping generalizations about male and female sexuality: Men have high sex drives; women barely want sex at all. Men are visual; women are emotional. Men will watch pornography; women will fantasize about their wedding day too much. While men and women are certainly psychologically, biologically, and even spiritually different in God's design for the sake of complementarity, the differences are portrayed as far too stark and become the focus *instead* of complementarity. Qualities shared by both sexes—such as desire, temptation, virginity, and sin—felt as if they were placed in either the "male" or the "female" box.

As I've previously mentioned, the only things I had heard about pornography were that it was wrong and that it was a "man's struggle." In my mind, it was in the "male" box. I went to many conferences and retreats where the guys and girls were separated, and the guys received a talk about pornography, while we received a talk on identity, worth, modesty, or emotional chastity. These topics are necessary and fruitful when done well, but the topic of sexuality was often addressed with us only regarding virginity and protecting men's minds. I remember one youth conference in high school in particular where this happened, and the female speaker (who had given a great talk on femininity and identity) then encouraged us to pray for our brothers in Christ, because they were in the other room learning about how "they can fight for us and honor us," and that pornography is a battle unique to men that is an uphill climb.

I sat cross-legged in the middle of a crowd of girls in the midst of my own uphill climb and felt like a phony—or worse, a monster. I felt, at that time and several others, that I didn't fit into the "woman box" very well when it came to sexuality, but I certainly didn't fit in the "male box." What's dangerous is that when you're made to feel like an outcast solely because of sexual sin, that feeling of "outcast" bleeds into other aspects of your femininity as well. It slowly but surely makes you feel as if your identity as a woman is damaged, compromised, or even ruined.

I read and heard from many sources promoting chastity that men struggled with pornography because they are visual and have higher sex drives. On the other hand, I was told that my fight for virtue would be primarily emotional, that I would have to curb my romantic fantasies and an overwhelming desire for a relationship. While I certainly needed emotional chastity, as all of us do, I never once heard in middle or high school, from any of these trusted sources, that a woman could become addicted to pornography. The feeling of being an anomaly deepened and so did my inherent discomfort with my sexuality in the first place. While those feelings and lies deepened, so did the need to reason with my addiction and hide it.

I don't think it's false that a large majority of men are visually triggered at higher levels than women are; I think the mistake is in the generalizations. I still receive comments on podcast episodes or articles, where I'm very clear about my own story or about my work, that go something like this: "Men's porn is visual; women's is emotional," or "Women struggle with romance and fantasy but not porn," or even "Maybe women do get addicted to porn, but men struggle waaaaaay more. The Church should put its energy where the real problem is." These are paraphrases of real comments and feedback I've received, and it's hard not to feel like the girl in the crowd at that conference again when I read them. Telling women (and men!) what sins they can and cannot struggle with purely based on gender is both counterproductive and proving to just be *false*. It capitulates the shame that is already so engrained in sexual sin.

Further, refusing to acknowledge the reality of female sexual sin and how sexual desire can become disordered sends the message that women don't have desires *at all*. Constantly hearing about how men have higher sex drives and therefore need more help controlling themselves can make women feel as if their desire doesn't matter, is embarrassing, or is even dangerous because male desire is so often referenced regarding their capacity to sin. Women having stunted, shameful, or fearful attitudes about their sexual desire doesn't just inhibit their ability to actively respond to their sin and weakness but also prevents them from fully experiencing the joy of their sexuality, particularly in marriage. If women don't have permission to desire as teenagers, they won't feel permission to desire as adults or when they get married; it's not a switch that can suddenly be flipped on. Desire should be affirmed in *both* men and women, and encouragement should be given to both on not how to *control* their desire but how to embrace it according to their state in life.

The development of the pornography industry, however, *did* take gender differences and female desire into account, and it now preys heavily on the female imagination as well as men's visual tendencies. In a 2009 study conducted by psychologists to evaluate both men's and women's sexual arousal responses to pornography, it was reported that while men attributed arousal to the attractiveness of the actresses and actors involved, women attributed their arousal to their ability to imagine themselves as the female in the video.[2] This shows that men and women can be addicted to the same visual material but *for different reasons.* Writing off the reality of women becoming addicted to pornography because it's "visual" not only writes off the other forms of pornography that are readily available for consumption but also makes yet another unnecessary—and unfactual—generalization. Essentially, it lacks nuance. In addition, the same study observed that these stereotypes played a role in the female reaction to visual pornography: "Because women may feel more self-conscious in their response to sexual stimuli due to societal expectations, they may try to inhibit their responses to match socialized gender roles in which women do not display high levels of sexual response."[3] It seems that secular culture, as well as the field of psychology, has recognized the addictions of women for a few decades now, but people of faith seem hesitant to do so. Further, both men and women are incredibly susceptible to pornography addiction solely because of what some clinicians and researchers call the "'triple A' influence" (accessibility, affordability, anonymity).[4] The privacy, free cost, and constant access online pornography provides made the struggles of both men *and* women skyrocket.

The generalizations that I encountered weren't limited to just pornography. Masturbation, while not a large part of my addiction but an *incredibly* large issue among women, also went unaddressed or was characterized as a "guy problem." Many women, myself included, had discovered masturbation *years* before it was even explained to them. It doesn't help that when it *is* finally explained to them, they're only told that "boys struggle with this." Within my nonprofit organization alone, a higher percentage of women struggle with masturbation than with pornography.

I think people shy away from explaining pornography and masturbation, especially to young women, out of fear. Maybe it's a fear of their own sin or past; a fear of letting go of the ideal of virginal, spotless women; or a fear of causing a problem instead of preventing one. I can't tell you how many times I've been "censored" in front of teen girls for even mentioning the word *pornography* when speaking about chastity and sexual sin. I literally had a parish cancel a talk the week I'm writing this because there was nervousness about addressing pornography with teenagers of both genders. While I completely support the rights of parents as primary educators and think the topic should always be addressed with their consent and support, I've found it contradictory that teenage girls can be in an environment, with the awareness and permission of their parents, where sex, virginity, and chastity are all addressed but pornography isn't allowed to be—usually for fear of something like girls "going home and looking it up." First of all, I've heard the stories of dozens upon dozens of women recovering from pornography and masturbation addictions at the time I'm writing this, and not one of them has ever attributed their first exposure to looking up pornography after its mentioned by a trusted voice in the Church trying to warn them against its use. Second, if we're going to address chastity with high-school-aged girls and teach them the sacredness of sex, they need to know that there are more ways to be irreverent toward that sacredness than just by being sexually active—teenage boys are taught this. The chastity message can't be gendered to the point of being incomplete for one of those genders, especially not out of fear.

One of the most harmful messages that I received, along with many other women, from purity culture was regarding virginity. Its link to pornography addiction and sexual sin may not seem obvious at first, but it's incredibly telling.

Idolizing Virginity

While I didn't lose my virginity before marriage, the mountain of shame I've seen piled on women who did has deeply affected how I go about my work. In several women's stories, it was a pornography addiction that led them to sexual activity in the first place, or on the flip side, becoming sexually active led them to seek a high in pornography when they weren't with a partner. Both loss of virginity and pornography addiction carry deep shame, in both men and women, but the shame in both perpetuates the cycle and keeps people in hiding.

I was sitting on a panel at a retreat for high school girls about a year ago, answering anonymous questions submitted by retreat participants, when a question about premarital sex came up. This took a turn toward discussing preserving virginity. One of the women sitting on the panel talked about saving sex for marriage and then said, "If you save your virginity, it's the most beautiful gift you can give to your future husband." I knew that many of the messages that I and the women around me had received about virginity were harmful, but that statement made it suddenly click: we were told that virginity is the greatest gift we have to give in a marriage, and that without it, we'll be damaged goods. My virtue could be collapsed into one quality, and if I didn't have it, then nothing else mattered—not my life's journey so far, my inherent human dignity, or the redemption of Christ from my sin.

On multiple occasions, one image I encountered in purity-related talks and books was a depiction of a man and woman on their wedding day. As they're standing at the altar, vowing themselves to one another, all of their sexual partners from the past come up and take the hands of the bride or groom, forming a chain trailing behind them as they look in shame at each other. It's a deeply disturbing image, attempting to illustrate that if you have sexual experiences before marriage, they will inhibit you from promising yourself fully to your spouse. Not only is it a disturbing image, but also it's a *false* one. First, the sacrament of marriage is one of the most tangible examples of "love cover[ing] a multitude of sins," as 1 Peter 4:8 says. While marriage doesn't wash your sins away, Jesus *does*, and living in his forgiveness is meant to free us from a fear of our past. If we're truly striving to trust in his mercy, we don't have a chain of past sexual partners interrupting his plan for our life, whether it involves marriage or not. We repent, we receive absolution, we forgive others as we've been forgiven, and we move forward in hope.

This isn't to say that the natural consequences of our sins get washed away when our sins do, but it is to say that those consequences are not more powerful than the grace of God. Having multiple sexual partners inherently creates memories and attachments that can be incredibly painful to let go of. Particularly regarding marriage, vowing your life to one person means embracing them along with their history and committing to pursuing Christ together even in the midst of brokenness. One of my friends who was not a virgin when she got married spoke about this beautifully when we were both engaged. She expressed to me, "I don't know what my wedding night will be like, what the consequences of my past will be, or if I'll be too triggered. But I know I'll be with my husband no matter what happens, and that's enough." What a stunning example of the safety and hope of a holy marriage, no matter either spouse's past. She trusted that her husband would be with her in her humanity and they would see it through together.

At the core of the problematic image of the couple at the altar, along with all the other messages about virginity, is that it treats sexuality as the only gift you give in a vocation. I've written about this in other contexts, but it bears repeating: the greatest gift any woman or man has to give in a marriage is *themselves*. My friend's simple wisdom is a testament to this; she trusted that the "gift of self," as Pope St. John Paul II popularized, would be present between her and her new husband, no matter what. I recognize that no one intended to cause shame and pain in women particularly by saying something to the contrary; many people probably didn't even feel they were saying something contrary to the truth about our dignity in the first place. But how hearts receive messages and the intent of the messenger are two very different things, and I know I'm not the only heart that received messages on virginity this way—not by far.

There's a fine line to walk when it comes to talking about the particulars of living out chastity, especially when you're single, and virginity is perhaps the finest of the lines. Virginity is an incredible gift, and it's a gift we should certainly encourage young people to strive to preserve. But to hinge the worth of a person's sexuality on whether they've successfully done so is a mistake, and it's in no way an accurate portrayal of the mercy of God. Beyond that, sex within marriage is much more than just giving your virginity; it's a complete gift of *self*, and it's lifelong—not just one time. Further, this idolization gives almost *zero* provision and compassion to women who don't lose their virginity by choice. Victims of rape and sexual assault have felt truly irredeemable in conversations like this, for a heinous crime committed *against* them.

The deeper message here, however, is that women—who have received the brunt of the virginity message—have been somewhat conditioned to see their sexuality as valuable only insofar as it's *perfect*. The emphasis on preserving virginity has made preservation the name of the game for women's sexuality, full stop. We're taught to preserve ourselves from defilement in body and soul, while men are almost *expected* to become defiled at some point. This is not healthy for either gender. While the expectation that men will sexually sin one day is perhaps discouraging, it at least gives them permission to struggle. What the message of preservation and a near perfectionism for women does is increase the sense of shame if we *do* fall. The musician Audrey Assad once said, in her own testimony regarding pornography addiction, that "although men and women alike struggle with pornography addiction, for the most part men are in jail together. . . . While for the most part women are locked into individual cells in the same prison."[5] By saying this, I in no way wish to downplay the shame men experience but rather want to illustrate the unique isolation women experience—and believe me, it is definitely experienced.

If a woman has lost her virginity, she has not lost her inherent worth as a daughter of God, nor has she lost her inherent worth if she falls into pornography, masturbation, or other sexual sins. The word that continually comes to mind when I think of what needs to change—how to change the narrative from one of fear to one of hope and mercy—is *refinement*. We have to recognize that we're not born with perfect sexuality, and every moment regarding it from then on is either damaging it or keeping it intact. Our goal is not preservation of sexuality, including virginity, but rather a continual *refining*—allowing "grace to perfect nature," as St. Thomas Aquinas said.[6] If we believe "perfect sexuality" is within our reach, if we behave well enough, we're completely missing the necessity of grace. Holiness is not won by living on the defense, continually "preserving" what we have by batting away sin. Instead, holiness is something we obtain by the grace of God through living on a kind of offense—by striving for virtue, falling, repenting, and abandoning ourselves to God's mercy and beginning again. We're a piece of rock being chiseled—refined—into a work of art, not a statue trying to keep ourselves from being shattered. We face the attacks head-on and find our merit in Christ's victory over them, not in our ability to avoid the adversaries and falls altogether. As St. Josemaría Escrivá simply stated, "A saint is a sinner who keeps trying." If our only attitude regarding sexuality is one of white-knuckled control in which one mistake means our complete downfall, we miss the joyful magnanimity that comes from overcoming weakness by God's grace. I believe that, especially as access to pornography and a sexualized culture begin to develop, the tone has to change to this attitude of refinement.

Finally, in most talks or Church-led conversations about chastity, I heard a repeated message of reaching a certain level of perfection before meeting "the one." I could probably write a whole book about how the phrase "the one" gets misconstrued, but I'll focus on the issue at hand: many times, speakers or people in leadership gave a nod to female sexual sin, saying that if you've lost your virginity, "you can start over again," but that ultimately, we needed to "be completely satisfied with Jesus" before we would find a husband. Sometimes this message was taken so far as to assert that God *intentionally wouldn't bring "the one"* until we were satisfied.

At first glance, this message seems not only true but also convicting. We absolutely should focus on our own growth in virtue and make sure we're in a healthy place to pursue a romantic relationship. But to be completely satisfied in Jesus means, quite simply, that you're dead. Further, hearing that message as someone battling addiction makes the vocation of marriage seem impossible. An addiction to pornography and/or masturbation makes it blatantly obvious that you're *not* fully satisfied in Christ, just like every other human being still breathing. Couple that with a temptation to despair or the feeling that your addiction is insurmountable and you have a very convincing lie that marriage just isn't an option for you.

The complex issue of readiness for relationship while struggling with addiction will be addressed in a later chapter, but statements like this don't seem to give any room for complexity, and they make marriage seem like a trophy that you win on the other side of perfection. Marriage was instituted as a sacrament to give grace to spouses to be refined and become saints together, not as a reward for the sinless. Further, to attribute this message to God—that he intentionally withholds necessary things for our journey to heaven until we reach a certain undefined level of satisfaction—proves harmful instead of convicting in the long run. There's a way to prepare to love a spouse well without feeling that their arrival, which may never occur, is based on how well you prepare.

Rephrasing the Chastity Message

I am convinced that what is necessary, especially when speaking to young people in the Church, isn't a "new" teaching of chastity; the truth of the virtue and what constitutes sexual sin is objective. Instead, what's needed is a "rephrasing" of our existing messages regarding chastity—a delivery that takes into account the increasing societal pressures young people face, that recognizes the sexuality of women, and that *always* places its end in Jesus Christ, not in our own actions. The Church should educate men and women on chastity and sexual sin equally, respectful of differences, but always rooting the message in one of hope—that Jesus has paid the price for our sin, that *there is nothing his mercy cannot redeem*, and that our only true happiness lies in loving him and living virtuously. This doesn't give young people permission to sin liberally and presume on mercy but rather allows them to see their shortcomings in sexuality as a place where every human is in need of God, not a place where they're expected to be perfect from day one. We need leaders teaching chastity with *nuance* and a knowledge that the human psyche and relationships are complex, made only more so by the ever-changing attitudes on sexuality present in our culture. We no longer live in a world where only female sexuality is exploited for men's pleasure—*everyone* is being exploited: men, women, and children alike. If we want to influence the present culture for the better, we have to first acknowledge the effects of it on *all* members of the Body of Christ. In light of this, the gendering of sexual sin needs to come to an end. Don't gender the problem, gender the solution; in other words, how men and women *heal* from sexual sin will be different because healing will happen through coming into a renewed and redeemed sense of their masculinity or femininity. The categorization of sins, however, is evidently both false *and* harmful.

One of my friends put it quite simply and charitably when we were recording a podcast about well-intentioned yet misleading messages on chastity (idolizing virginity in particular): "We're just broken people, speaking to broken people, trying to teach them not to be broken." First, I think my friend's statement unknowingly hit the nail on the head: we're trying to teach people how *not* to be broken when it comes to sexuality instead of teaching them *where* to take their inevitable brokenness. The focus has to be on the redemption of Christ, not the virtue of the presenter. Some of the most powerful presentations on chastity or *any* virtue that I've witnessed have come from a speaker who is willing to admit their brokenness. Testimony, I believe, is a far better teacher than mere presentation; it's definitely more impactful than presenting one's self, marriage, or life as the standard.

Regarding women and pornography addiction in particular, perhaps we're just learning to "phrase" the struggle to begin with. I know now, through my current work, that I was not the only girl feeling like a confused, dirty outsider in chastity talks. Equipping young women with not just stories of sin, healing, and redemption but also context and support for their struggle akin to what young men have received in this arena will create healthier women and a healthier Church.

3

HOW WE GOT HERE: THE HISTORY OF THE PORNOGRAPHY INDUSTRY

To a great extent the level of any civilization
is the level of its womanhood. When a man
loves a woman, he has to become worthy of
her. The higher her virtue, the more noble
her character, the more devoted she is to
truth, justice, goodness, the more a man has
to aspire to be worthy of her. The history of
civilization could actually be written in terms
of the level of its women.

–Fulton Sheen

The myth that women don't struggle with sexual compulsion or
can't be addicted to pornography didn't begin with purity culture. While it may be one of the most unpleasant places to go,
understanding the history of the pornography industry—how it

developed in the type of content it produces and how it began preying on the particulars of female sexuality and psyche—can help us leave behind the notion that porn is aimed toward only men, once and for all.

The Beginning of Erotic Depiction

Erotic depictions, or art meant to elicit sexual reactions, have been present in different civilizations and cultures for thousands of years. The oldest surviving erotic depiction we have is believed to be about twenty-eight *thousand* years old. It's called the Venus of Willendorf, a clay figure of a busty, curvy naked woman that was potentially used for fertility rites or "sex festivals."[1] The concept of creating art solely for such practices is disturbing, but it proves to us what the purpose of erotic depictions has *always* been: an encouragement of a basely carnal sexuality instead of one that embraces sacredness and love.

Another early example of pornography is the Kangjiashimenji Petroglyphs, which date back about four thousand years ago in northern China. The petroglyphs are almost-cartoonish images carved in stone, depicting a man demanding pleasure from several women bystanders.[2] These are far from the only early erotic depictions that are preserved for our viewing today; the Babylonians and Greeks, with more refined art forms, continued the trend, depicting more and more graphic sexual acts.

One resource for early pornographic depictions is Pompeii, famed for its destruction—and remarkable preservation—from an explosion from Mt. Vesuvius in AD 79. In Pompeii, historians have found a surplus of detailed early pornography that indicated an incredibly permissive sexual society—not uncommon among the Romans. Because of the depictions and other items preserved from the city, Pompeii has been understood to have had legal prostitution and practiced sex slavery.[3]

While multiple cultures involved male sex slavery as well, in most historical understandings, women drew the short end of the stick. In Pompeii and other Roman cities, for instance, prostitutes were predominantly women who had been captured from conquests in other countries. Roman culture had a very permissive sexual culture for men, including a great deal of encouragement of male-on-male activity and relationships, but not so permissive for women, who were seen as sexually passive and subordinate. Some of the pornographic images depicted in these cultures would show women seemingly "in control" of the scene, but this was typically done for the sake of humor, knowing the opposite was true.[4]

What Pornography Tells Us

Seeing and learning about the sexual attitudes of earlier civilizations may cause us disgust, but it doesn't take much time to realize that sexuality in our culture is just as degraded. Sex slavery is an industry that is far from dead. In fact, it's thriving. In the United States alone, it's estimated that about fifteen thousand to fifty thousand women and children are forced into sexual slavery every year, though some studies have placed that number much higher, capping at 325,000.[5] We should be absolutely horrified at this number and be doing everything in our power to stop it, beginning with addressing our own attachments to pornography in *any* form or other behaviors that directly or indirectly feed the human-trafficking industry. In their documentary on the personal and societal harms of the porn industry, the nonprofit corporation Fight the New Drug cites that even in mainstream porn production, actors and actresses can be filmed against their will or sign contracts for jobs that don't describe what a producer ends up demanding of them.[6] The filmed content is then distributed without their consent, with little hope of it ever being taken down.

It's clear that even from ancient times, our attitudes about sexuality are depicted in what we're willing to portray publicly and consume. Pornography and sexualized content aren't just limited to porn sites for us, let alone cave walls; it's in movies, books, and advertisements. Women are *still* on the receiving end of a great deal of the brutality of the porn and sex-slavery industries. How, then, did women end up joining the demographic of addicts, when pornography is so degrading to women in the first place?

The Development of Modern Pornography

In early modern France, the philosopher Marquis de Sade wrote a major player in the development of erotic literature. It was an introductory piece to the public on the practices of BDSM, behaviors in sexuality that include bondage, discipline, sadism, and masochism.[7] While Marquis was eventually jailed primarily for practicing what he preached, the effects of his work last even to today, where works depicting BDSM, like *Fifty Shades of Grey*, aren't just books but are developed into movies.

The dawn of film brought pornography to the screen as early as the 1880s, though it grew more and more explicit over time. By the 1920s, what began as simply depicting naked women in film had advanced to far more graphic sexual acts akin to what pornography depicts today. During World Wars I and II, however, the porn industry lapsed, only to boom again when Hugh Hefner came on the scene.

In 1953, Hefner released the first *Playboy* magazine, with the famous tagline "Entertainment for Men" under the title. Over the years, a plethora of famous women have posed nude for *Playboy*, from Madonna to Pamela Anderson and Drew Barrymore. As the magazine rose in popularity, it became more and more of a career booster for women to pose for *Playboy* instead of something that could potentially damage them.

The Sexual Revolution and Feminism

The evolution of feminism has been written about extensively in other areas, but for our purposes, examining its connection to the sexual revolution, and thus the further development of the porn industry, is key. It's important to note here that I am not a historian, nor do I consider myself a feminist by modern definition or a scholar of feminism. However, I find myself in the tension that I believe many women find themselves in—feminism, particularly first-wave, won us rights and freedoms that we hold dear, but it's also contributed to mass confusion and destruction of what it means to be feminine in many respects. Also a major player in this tension between the boldness of modern feminism and the traditional role of housewife—both with their mishandling of female sexuality—was the lack of proper acknowledgment and catechesis on the role and dignity of women, and on sexuality in general on the part of the Church. Women felt, and sometimes still feel, confused about where exactly they truly live the fullness of God's call for them, and have not always seen the Church come to their defense when they most needed it to do so. Words like "subordination" and "submission," especially in the letters of St. Paul, have very different meanings than how many people have applied them throughout the centuries—it's the disordered forms of these words that I'm addressing. John Paul II, in addition to his *Theology of the Body*, made massive strides in affirming women's place in the Church and society, while also clarifying what it means to live authentically as a woman—what he called the "feminine genius." Properly speaking, the feminine genius includes submission, but under the pretense that we're submitting to a charitable, Christ-like love. As I said, entire books can and have been written on these topics, but for our purposes, focusing on the perspectives on female sexuality that feminism offered gives us great insight into both what women have suffered and how *not* to solve it.

After World Wars I and II, there was a cultural shift to emphasizing domestic life, with hardworking fathers, blissfully happy children, and perfectly put-together, demure mothers with not a hair out of place (if you want the perfect example, just watch one episode of *Leave It to Beaver*). I'm not knocking this portrayal as evil or wrong, but it gave no credence to what was brewing underneath—the growing influence of oversexualized and objectifying sources like *Playboy* and the rumblings of the sexual revolution.

Feminism also saw its resurgence around this time, after winning what's considered to be its "first wave" battles in the early twentieth century by earning women rights, such as the right to vote and own property. While these victories were massive, the focus of feminism turned in the 1950s and '60s precisely *toward* the portrayal of domestic life written above and made it its target. As the feminist writer and activist Betty Friedan drove home in her famous work *The Feminine Mystique*, the expectations and portrayals of society left many women feeling restricted. The restriction came from a question deep in women's hearts that Friedan isn't incorrect in articulating: "Is this all?" She also painfully yet beautifully called it "the ache that has no name." However, instead of finding the answer to our ache in the pursuit of heaven, Friedan and many other modern feminists turned toward merely changing the roles, perceptions, and opportunities of women, allowing the ache to become resentment. What was missing was the recognition that neither the domestic life nor the workforce—women's exterior lives—can solve the issues beneath the surface in our interior lives, or fix the sinfulness of both men and women.

This resentment was, and is, incredibly vicious. The philosopher and scholar Carrie Gress, in her work *The Anti-Mary Exposed*, points out that women's malcontent and resentment became an entry point for the temptation of the devil. Instead of upholding the beauty of femininity and domestic life while still working to generate positive change in society and the workforce regarding women's capabilities, gifts, or the respect due to our sexuality, women started to turn toward attacking the very things that make us women.[8]

As a manifestation of their resentment, women began to view themselves as men's competitors rather than partners.[9] Women turning to the competitive mindset, while riddled with problems and divisiveness, makes sense. Centuries of sexual objectification and violent demands of subordination became coupled with a societal expectation of perfection and subjection, and it became too much. Women were hurting, and they were angry, and so they sought to no longer be the ones drawing the short end of the stick, societally and sexually. The attack on traditional femininity and domestic life felt like a balm to those wounds, but they didn't actually solve the problems that may have been hiding under women's roles in society—one of them being the problem of oversexualization, or giving an unhealthy dominance to men instead of encouraging a charitable protection and stewardship in them. The sexual revolution was an opportune time to try to turn the tables.

Christianity, on the other hand, didn't seem to offer anything different to women; it offered no option to heal the anger and pain from oversexualization, objectification, and sexual suppression while also sometimes seeming to be the very source of demanding the perfect demure housewife. Women felt they were left with a choice when it came to true virtuous sexual expression: let the pattern continue or become men's competitors in both the sexual realm and the societal realm. Competition, in a way, became the new virtue worth pursuing—the one we thought would offer us the freedom we desired.

Choosing to Give In

In examining the history of the porn industry and the sociocultural contexts that developed within it, we see the tragedy is that it actually left women no choice but to stay victims. Just as pornography in early cultures depicted the attitudes and practices of the given people that produced it, our pornography and sexual activities portray *exactly* what we're doing and thinking when it comes to sexuality today.

As the award-winning journalist Peggy Orenstein states when addressing the porn industry: "The most efficient way [to get men off fast for profit] appears to be by eroticizing the degradation of women."[10] She couldn't be hitting it more on the nose. This degradation actually angered many notable feminists, such as Gloria Steinem, who opposed violent pornography in particular. Despite the influence and voice of Steinem and others, the oversexualization and sexual suppression of women didn't change post–sexual revolution; it was just given our stamp of approval. The sexual revolution wanted a sexuality unfettered by rules; it didn't work, and still doesn't, for something to be "off limits." Feminism, similarly, wanted competition, and that bled into every area of life —including beating men in their own game of degrading women.

Even more tragically, women have allowed their arousal to now be linked to abusive behaviors that are regularly depicted in porn. Orenstein continues in her observations: "In the study of behaviors in popular porn, nearly 90 percent of 304 random scenes contained physical aggression toward women, while close to half contained verbal humiliation. The victims nearly always responded neutrally or with pleasure."[11] Remembering that women are chiefly aroused by porn through their ability to imagine themselves as the women being depicted, it only makes sense that pornography would then inform their sexual preferences or behaviors in real life by making abuse, violence, and humiliation steadily more and more arousing. I have heard women's stories where they cannot have sex with a spouse without role-playing that they are being abused, because their sexual arousal has become so deeply linked to pornographic depictions. This is *devastating*—the very place where sex should feel safest and most affirming for both people becomes totally warped solely because of porn's influence. Porn doesn't just allow abuse; it makes it appealing and the norm. It's deeply heartbreaking, and it didn't change the problem of oversexualization and abuse of women throughout history; it only made it worse. Not only is sexual suppression and abuse eroticized for men through pornography, but it's also eroticized for women—a phenomenon that is perhaps unique and definitely detrimental to our culture.

I believe pornography found women in the tension that built up through the centuries, and came to a head in the twentieth century. The seemingly polar opposites of demure housewife—perfect on the exterior yet objectified behind the scenes—and the modern liberated woman—still sexualized but okay with it—seemed to be our only choices. The choice was to remain silently in the tiredness and objectification, or to go out and discover what unbridled sexuality could offer—what men seemed to always have access to all along. However, despite some of the promises of the sexual revolution, we could never truly become *like men* when it came to sexuality. Instead, the broken roles of both men and women would just become fetishized, and we would consent to it. The porn industry watched and knew this, there's no doubt. It knew that deep down in our feminine hearts, we wanted communion and relationships that thrive—romance, opportunity, *life*—and it offered the counterfeit. It knew that we were trying to reckon with years of abuse, often hidden, and widespread cultural objectification. It *knew* that women were tired, and it came to be a wolf in sheep's clothing. "The ache that has no name" became the target of the porn industry too—not just for secular feminism but for women of faith as well.

Unfortunately, as we can see clearly, unbridled sexuality has only resulted in *more* objectification, and sometimes women are the very people to do it to themselves. The violence toward and use of women sexually has not changed. The only thing that has changed is that *we* now give the green light to do it, and we *celebrate* it, calling it "liberation." At the same time, we've seen an increase in conversation about "consent" being the pinnacle virtue when it comes to sexual activity, as if consenting or not consenting can shut the Pandora's box we've opened.

It's brutal, because both Christianity and feminism, in my opinion, were on to something in that clash at the time of the sexual revolution. Christianity sought to protect the dignity of the human person, marriage, and sexuality, but did so in a way that was no longer completely compatible with a socioeconomically permanently changed world; it needed to recognize the capabilities of women beyond the home, especially after the world wars, and catechize on the sexuality of the human person in a way that could aptly and charitably respond to the growing sexual promiscuity of our culture. On the other hand, feminism was rightfully acknowledging the centuries of harmful forms of women, particularly in the sexual realm. The Church, in many ways, seemed to stay silent on these matters, and women didn't always know where to turn.

The pornography industry, along with other compulsions like masturbation and fantasy, provided a way out for faithful women caught in the in-between, like me. While we strive to "be in the world and not of it," as the Gospel of John alludes to, we are not immune to its shortcomings and attitudes. The pull of the "liberation" that sexual sin and compulsion promises, whether explicitly or implicitly through our oversexualized culture, is hard to completely ignore.

After the sexual revolution and with the beginning of internet porn, modern pornography, masturbation, and other sexual compulsions offered something—particularly for the Christian woman—that previous centuries never could: secrecy. The sexual ethic offered to us in secular culture, though depraved, at least acknowledged our sexuality in a way our churches did not. Pornography and masturbation can seemingly offer ways to recognize our sexuality without any cost to our image or others' perceptions of our faith and moral life. In a sneaky, conniving way, it offers some of the most twisted parts of the modern approach to sexuality without making a woman feel as if she's compromising or exposing herself publicly through her behavior with others. Some women experience a strange comfort in the secrecy porn, masturbation, and fantasy provide, but the shame after engaging in their behaviors tells a different story. The ache still remains, and we know in our heart of hearts that sin can never be the answer, no matter how many times we try.

Recovering the Ache

I've found that a major part of recovery for women is to accept and become present to that "ache that has no name." Betty Friedan, though I disagree with her vehemently on most of the topics she addressed, *did* have that correct. The question "Is this all?" will haunt every woman until she completes her journey on earth. The difference between the Betty Friedans and the St. Mary Magdalenes isn't that one group had the ache and the other didn't; it's that one looked to the world to solve her ache, and the other looked to Christ.

When women are recovering, that question comes back to them again as they look at their life riddled with sexual compulsion and shame: "Is this all?" The answer is no, it's not. But in order to truly heal, they have to hold that question in their hands and learn to take it to a different source than the one they've been seeking. They have to learn to recognize the long history of brutality toward and manipulation of women by the porn industry and its ancestors, and what a total counterfeit it is. While acknowledging what their sexual compulsions did to temporarily fill the ache, they have to rehabilitate it and take it to the feet of Jesus.

A massive part of female recovery is also learning to not believe the lies of the porn industry, secular society, *or* purity culture about their sexuality. Instead, recovering the ache inherent to their souls and focusing it on God gives them the grace to accept and bless their sexuality and sexual desires. They are no longer under the lies of suppression and ignorance, nor the ones of promiscuity, competition, and false liberation. The Church beautifully blesses and affirms the good of human sexuality in doctrine, even when some in the Church don't articulate that doctrine in the way they should. The ache is not something to take to a secret source to fill but rather something to be grateful for and surrender in *every* part of our lives—spiritually, socially, mentally, and sexually. Recovery comes only in recovering the ache too, not in suppressing it or giving consent to the endless cycle of exploitation. Only when our longing and desires, including sexual, are properly accepted and looked on with love can we cease to be prey for the trap of both suppression and the porn industry.

4
WAKING UP

Peter knows that he is known both in his love
and his treason: Lord, you know everything:
you know that I love you (Jn. 21:17).

–Hans Urs von Balthasar

My favorite part of giving talks at universities or events, hands-down, is the opportunity to have one-on-one conversations with women afterward. I've been humbled and honored to be the recipient of many brave and beautiful women's stories—sometimes I'm the first to ever hear them. One conversation I will never forget came after a talk I gave several months ago at a women's retreat in rural New Jersey, when a lovely young woman came and sat with me. She had a radiant smile, and after thanking me for the talk and sharing a bit more about herself, she said, "I want to admit to you, for the first time, that I am a pornography and masturbation addict, and *I am so tired*." Tears poured down her face as she said it, but her smile of relief remained, though she was clearly in pain from sharing her experience.

Tears sprang to my eyes too as a result, because the exhaustion she articulated and embodied in that moment is an experience many addicts in recovery resonate with. This young woman was remarkably devout, and she shared some insights from her journey with me. She was incredibly inspiring, but her exhaustion remained, and her devotion and encounters with God only increased it.

The feeling of exhaustion, I believe, comes from a place of feeling hypocritical or two-faced. A wise priest once told my husband, "If you don't feel at least a little like a hypocrite, your standards aren't high enough," which I tend to agree with. The devil doesn't spend much time attacking or tempting those whom he already has in his grasp. But exhaustion comes when the hypocrisy feels overwhelming and it seems as though your unwanted sexual behaviors are inhibiting every other part of your life. Thoughts like "If they only knew," or "My prayer means nothing because I'm in this sinful pattern," or "God must be perpetually disappointed in me" echo constantly in the mind of a person who's hitting the wall of their behaviors over and over again.

Despite the pain of hitting that wall and the exhaustion that comes with feeling hypocritical and trapped, it's a necessary part of recovery. St. Paul articulates the struggle with oneself in his letter to the Romans: "For I do not do the good I want, but I do the evil I do not want" (Rom 7:19). I don't get concerned when I see this attitude arise in the women I speak with or accompany because it's a sign they're waking up. They're seeing how their unwanted sexual behaviors—whether it's pornography use, masturbation, lustful fantasies, or promiscuity—are not truly fulfilling the desires they have for their life and are preventing them from living as they want to. Oftentimes, though, this process of exhaustion with oneself takes time, and you almost always have to begin by *wanting* to be exhausted with yourself, instead of feeling apathetic toward your behavior.

Putting Distance

I don't remember a particular moment that I hit a wall with my pornography addiction. I didn't hit "rock bottom," per se. Instead, I woke up one morning with a conviction. It was my senior year of high school, and I woke up with an overwhelming desire to get rid of my smartphone. I promptly drove myself to the Verizon store, where I stood in line to get help behind an elderly woman with her daughter. The woman was asking for a simpler phone, something "that flips open and I can push the buttons." When the faithful Verizon attendant approached me to ask what I was looking for that day, I said, "I'll have what she's having."

To the surprise of *multiple* faithful Verizon attendants, I walked out of the store that day with my number ported to a flip phone. Once it was in my hand, I finally had time to catch up with what I had just done—and why.

I was becoming increasingly exhausted with how quickly accessible pornography was to me, especially through my phone. I had tried disabling internet access, but I was able to then download apps to compensate. This isn't uncommon; it's part of the self-deception and loss of willpower we covered in the first chapter. My phone was glued to my hand, like most teenagers, and that meant access to pornography went around with me everywhere too. While media and technology's role in addiction will be addressed in a later chapter, it's worth noting here that the creation of the smartphone has been absolutely detrimental to addicts trying to recover. Living in a world that increasingly encourages smartphones just to function—ordering at restaurants, paying for parking—while desperately trying to just get *distance* between you and porn for a second feels nearly impossible. Remember that "triple A influence" that clinicians are concerned about—accessibility, affordability, and anonymity. Smartphones are perhaps the greatest provider of all three when it comes to pornography.

This is why the "dumb phone" seemed like the most viable option, and why—by the grace of God—I was able to go find one in an almost frenzied state of mind. I was angry about what pornography was doing to the hearts and minds of young people (men, mostly; I still thought I was an anomaly), and I was noticing what it was doing to my heart and mind too. My thoughts were incredibly difficult to control, and moments of high negative emotion—anger,

sadness, loneliness, and the like—sent me to pornography to regu-
late myself. My exhaustion with myself was beginning.

I have a particular memory of my intense anger toward pornography showing itself two years earlier in high school. Toward
the end of chemistry class, a guy classmate of mine randomly asked
if I had read *Fifty Shades of Grey*. I was disgusted by his question
and insulted that he would think that I would read it in the first
place. My reaction was disproportionate, mostly because of an
unwillingness to admit to myself, at the time, that by reading and
watching the content I had, I wasn't doing any better than reading
Fifty Shades.

"No, that's porn," I said blatantly to my classmate.

His reply was typical: "Yeah, what's wrong with that?"

A debate ensued where I tried for days in on-and-off
conversations while walking halls and sitting in the back of
chemistry class to convince this classmate that pornography was
wrong. People who know me know I'm more than a sucker for a
debate on just about anything, but I couldn't seem to convince
my classmate. I argued with fervor, so convicted of the harms of
pornography, all while secretly hiding an attachment to it myself.
I can't remember how active my addiction was at that point in my
life; perhaps I was experiencing an easier period of time where my
compulsions weren't so strong, so I felt I was "done." Whatever the
reason, I didn't link my anger with pornography to myself, at least
not consciously. Subconsciously, I believe I did. Somewhere deep
down, I was arguing with myself.

Admitting Addiction

I also don't consciously remember a singular moment in which I
finally *admitted* that I was addicted to pornography. Perhaps it was
the realization of how many years it had been, what felt like an
intractable influence on my thoughts, or a sense of guilt and shame
that I could no longer dismiss. It felt more like a dawning—a
harsh, just, and painful one: I was addicted, and I needed to be

done. I had the sense that it would ruin my life if I didn't get it under control.

It was that push that sent me to get a dumb phone that day—the feeling that my addiction was a monster, hiding in the dark, who was continually gaining influence and power over me. If I didn't *do* something, it felt as if I would become a monster eventually too. I was beginning to fear that my capability to love well and to experience attraction without lust were both irreparably damaged.

I've noticed a hesitation in many men and women I've spoken with to admit that they're addicted. Sometimes it comes from a misunderstanding of what constitutes addiction. They're judging it based purely on frequency, which for women especially isn't the best gauge because of our hormones and cycle of fertility. (More on that later!) More than that, it comes from a fear that if they admit they're addicted, they have to face the truth of what that means. Ironically, it's the thing people fear the most—admitting addiction—that actually is the beginning of freedom. It certainly was in my case. There's a reason why AA or other twelve-step models have you say it right off the bat: "My name is so-and-so, and I'm an addict."

John 8:32 says, "You will know the truth, and the truth will set you free." This includes the truth of our sin and weakness. Admitting to the fact that you're addicted doesn't give the addiction more power; in fact, it slowly starts to chip away at the power it has over you. Addictions thrive in darkness and secrecy, and admitting to them—even just to yourself at first—is a way of shining a high beam on them. Switching phones was my way of admitting addiction to myself; this was a problem that I now needed a lot of help with, and I couldn't get free by continuing on the same path.

One of the first questions I ask any addict I speak with now is "What are you willing to do?" People reveal a lot about their desire for freedom in their answers. If they look away and stammer, then I know that perhaps they have a few more walls to hit before the upswing begins. If they say "Anything," I know they're exhausted and truly ready to be done. Along with admitting their addiction, they aren't afraid of admitting that they've tried doing it on their own, and they know they can't anymore. Ultimately they recognize the end of their own striving for solutions and are ready to do the most difficult, painful, brave, and healing thing there is: surrender and explore their own story with the love of God to accompany them. The young woman at the beginning of this chapter encapsulated this perfectly. Her exhaustion was a testament to her desire to surrender, which is a testament to the hope of her freedom.

Now, it's important to note that being "done" can take months, weeks, or even years. Recovery from any addiction is a marathon, not a sprint. But being *willing* to undergo the process—no matter how long it takes—is necessary to truly begin. In many ways, the journey of recovery never completely ends; there's always more healing to be done. This isn't meant to be discouraging; rather, it's an invitation to experience the love of God at an increasing depth, and that's not only true for addicts. I don't believe we can receive complete healing from our woundedness and shame on this side of heaven. We can certainly be delivered from their influence over our lives, but until those wounds are glorified in heaven alongside the wounds of Christ, parts of them can still cause pain and confusion even after we've received deep levels of healing.

While purchasing the dumb phone was the beginning of perhaps the first phase of my healing, it wasn't enough to keep me free. It gave me space from the pull of pornography being in my back pocket, but other devices and my own thoughts still provided plenty of opportunity to continue in my habits. Taking the first step, though, toward getting myself out of the routine that allowed pornography to stay a part of my life was crucial.

Honesty with God

The second step came through a simple birthday present. Shortly after purchasing my dear old dumb phone, a close friend of mine gave me a journal with a lovely letter in the first few pages. It's sitting next to me as I write this, and his words are still tender and wise beyond his then-teenage years: "It is my hope that this journal would be a place where you're free to openly express yourself—the good, artistic, and the painful and ugly as well . . . my greatest prayer for you is that you would continue to fall deeply in love with the person of Christ, and that you might learn what it truly means for Jesus to be enough for you." This friend didn't know of my struggle with pornography, not until later. But that journal was a place where I truly learned to begin to be honest with God.

I began journaling regularly, which gave me a rhythm of prayer I hadn't found before. With the rhythm of prayer came a new accountability and awareness of my own sin and weakness, as is typically the case with journaling. Early on in that journal, my entries seem superficial and immature at times: I talked to God about your average high school drama, boys, and questioning college decisions. But as the pages go on, I start to see how God began to give me the grace to be honest with myself and with him. What I refer to as my "lust problem" in the first few entries later is called what it is, and the feelings of shame and despair that came from the struggle are finally articulated. I had a place to talk about how I felt dirty, worthless, hopeless . . . and I had a place to beg for a way out. There was no more sweeping under the rug, no more hiding—at least not with him. The Person who mattered most finally knew, or had always known; it was me who now knew that he knew.

Soon after receiving the journal, I wrote my first article for a women's website called theYoungCatholicWoman on women's pornography addiction. I was eighteen when I wrote it and still living at home. This is how my parents were finally tipped off to my struggle. When I wrote it, I think I believed that I would never fall to pornography again and "was on the other side." Flipping through my journal entries, I can see there were several moments when I thought this. But for every moment I was convinced I was through, there were more moments where I fell into pornography use or fantasizing. The slow process of learning honesty with God meant that I finally had to reconcile with the fact that I couldn't just "pray" this away. I had given lust a stronghold in my life, and it would take significant effort to get it out. There's one entry in particular, dated in the summer before I left for college, that really finally articulated my bondage and pain: "I am so ashamed, Lord. I try and try, but I can't beat this. . . . I don't want to be a prisoner to this lust. What do I do? How do I get out? Where did this come from—this need to escape? I want none of it. It just brings loneliness and shame. I want to be good, Lord—holy—but this is getting in my way over and over and over."

That's how it felt, that I could run toward virtue and holiness all I wanted and give it my all but that the obstacle of lust and pornography would continually obstruct my path and I would never reach the goal. I felt that at every moment I would finally hit a stride, I would fall faster and harder than before. However, while my newfound honesty with God brought about crushing realizations, those realizations felt raw and true—and that truth was freeing. My friend gave me that journal to articulate, as he said, the "good, artistic, and the painful and ugly," and articulate the ugly I did. Looking back, I can see the good and artistic *within* the painful and ugly. Not only is this journal where I can trace my journey toward freedom from pornography, but it's also where I can see a tangible beginning to a deeper love story with Christ, a love story I had resisted out of fear.

One of the questions I've gotten frequently when sharing my testimony is, "How do I begin bringing this addiction to God in prayer?" There's a hesitation in many women I've journeyed and spoken with, and it's a hesitation I am personally familiar with. Bringing this particular sin, or sexual sin in general, to God is easier said than done. Quite frankly, it sucks.

I can't claim to know how men's hearts operate before God, on a general or individual level. But I do know that the feminine heart feels the lies we've discussed from purity culture—that she must have a perfect, unblemished sexuality—most potently in the presence of Our Lord. Woman images Christ's bride, the Church, in a unique way, and woman bears the same image as his Mother, who *was* spotless and unblemished by the grace of God. In our femininity we're also able to experience the masculinity of Jesus very potently. To bring a sexual sin before the Lord feels like the terror of bringing it to not just a man but *the* Man. We feel the shame of "not being woman enough" for him, and it's crippling if we allow it to be.

In order to truly bring our sexual sin as women before God, it takes a transformation in more areas than just our sexuality. We have to begin to believe in the core of our being that God is not ashamed of us, not *scandalized* by our sin. He had knowledge of it before time began and brought us into existence anyway. We are intended, known, and redeemed—and therefore worthy. Once again, it takes a lifelong ascent of faith to believe this, and it requires a willingness to be transformed.

There are several examples in the gospels of women who allow their identity to be transformed by Jesus, and several of them are directly related to sexual sin. My personal favorite is John 8, when a woman caught in adultery is brought before Jesus. The passage goes as follows:

> Then the scribes and the Pharisees brought a woman who had been caught in adultery and made her stand in the middle. They said to him, "Teacher, this woman was caught in the very act of committing adultery. Now in the law, Moses commanded us to stone such women. So what do you say?" They said this to test him, so that they could have some charge to bring against him. Jesus bent down and began to write on the ground with his finger. But when they continued asking him, he straightened up and said to them, "Let the one among you who is without sin be the first to throw a stone at her." Again he bent down and wrote on the ground. And in response, they went away one by one, beginning with the elders. So he was left alone with the woman before him. Then Jesus straightened up and said to her, "Woman, where are they? Has no

one condemned you?" She replied, "No one, sir." Then
Jesus said, "Neither do I condemn you. Go, [and] from
now on do not sin any more." (Jn 8:3–11)

This passage was deeply impactful in my recovery. The woman
caught in adultery is like any human being caught in sin, really,
but for women who are trapped in sexual sin in particular, she
lends a tender image. Her sin is exposed, out there in the open for
Christ and others to know. Exposure like that is a porn addict's
worst nightmare. Jesus not only dismisses those who wish to punish
her by establishing a convicting solidarity between them and the
woman based on the fact that they're all sinners but also dismisses
any punishment in general. He is the *only one* who reserves the
right, out of his justice, to admonish this woman for her sin. But
he doesn't. Instead, he says he doesn't condemn her, and he sends
her on her way with the instruction to sin no more.

When women especially are able to see that *this* is how Our
Lord will treat them in their sexual sin, there's an unshakable sense
of peace and healing. He only wants exposure of sin before him
for the sake of redemption, not for humiliation or destruction.
One entire session of our recovery group model is now dedicated
to reflecting on this passage. Jesus saying "Neither do I condemn
you. Go [and] from now on do not sin any more" isn't just true
for the woman in John 8; it's true for every woman who is willing
to go before him in her fear, shame, and sin. Jesus even calls her
"woman," not to be impersonal but to set her as a prototype, and
to tell her that she's not an adulteress but a *woman* created in his
image and likeness. He gives her what her accusers tried so hard
to take away by solely defining her by a moment of wrongdoing.
Jesus doesn't just dismiss the accusation; he affirms the woman's
identity as *woman*, not as an adulteress. He invites her to remember
her beginning.

However terrifying bringing our sin to the Lord may feel, he
always does this: without fail and with such tenderness, he affirms
our identity as a beloved son or daughter, a man or woman created
in his image and likeness, with unimaginable and precious dignity

that can never be taken away from us. We may try to define ourselves by our sin, but he never does.

Exhaustion Leads to Surrender

Part of why I see this feeling of exhaustion or hypocrisy as a hallmark of recovery is that it can lead to surrender. The second step in the twelve-step recovery model is "coming to believe in a higher Power that can restore [you] to sanity."[1] Recognizing the interior battle for what it is—defeating, exhausting, and painful—can help lead you to surrender yourself to the only Person who can be truly victorious. While honesty with God is pivotal, it doesn't mean we're surrendering to him and believing he can help us.

When I left for college, I had spent the last several months of high school getting a lot of my behaviors, I believed, "under control." Despite my increased honesty with God, I hadn't yet surrendered myself to his help and a true belief that an end could come. I had a pretty narrow "preventative" mindset of recovery: I focused on what *I* could *do* in order to *prevent* myself from getting to pornography instead of addressing why I *wanted* or sought pornography in the first place, and opening up those places in my heart to the Lord. As Jay Stringer says, "Lust exposes your demand to be filled. But if you listen to your lust, it will reveal a holy desire for belonging . . . the journey out of unwanted behavior begins by recognizing that your struggles may be the most honest dimension of your life. Your sexual struggles reveal your wounds, but they also reveal the trafficked longings of your heart."[2] Getting behaviors "under control" is not a good recipe for long-term recovery because your control is human and limited. It took a few different lessons for me to actually learn that. Instead, allowing your exhaustion to lead to deeper surrender to Jesus *instead* of control, and allowing him to touch and heal the most tender and painful parts of your experiences and memory, sets the break that caused the behaviors in the first place. In the realm of faith, surrender doesn't mean defeat; it means entrusting the victory to whom it belongs.

The Red Lizard

My exhaustion with myself and my addictive behaviors finally drove me to surrender in my first semester of college. I was on a small Catholic campus, and my feeling of being a total hypocrite only intensified. As I took advantage of the tools my school offered to deepen my interior life—whether in class, opportunities for daily Mass and adoration, or a faithful community of like-minded men and women—I felt inherently prevented from truly growing because of my secret sin.

Part of what pushed me over the edge was meeting my first boyfriend, who treated me with a respect and gentleness I had never encountered from a guy I was interested in before. As our friendship started to build into a relationship, I felt my shame over pornography painfully increase. It haunted most of my interactions with him and constantly nagged at the back of my mind. The thought that he was too pure and I was dirty, or that if he only knew, he would run away, was crippling at times.

One night during a late-night study session, I told him about my favorite book at the time, *The Great Divorce* by C. S. Lewis. The story follows a ghost's journey from hell into heaven, through which Lewis illustrates the different sins and vices common to humanity. There's a particular chapter that I recommend every human being read, about a ghost trying to journey into heaven with a red lizard wrapped around his shoulders. For Lewis, the red lizard represented lust. It chatters to the ghost that it keeps captive, and it weighs him down as he inches closer and closer to heaven. Lewis's character, who narrates, watches as the ghost encounters an angel who tells him he can't continue into heaven with the lizard. What ensues is a debate between the angel, who asks to kill the lizard, and the ghost who refuses to let go, insisting that if the lizard dies, he will also die.

I've yet to find a better representation of what lust is like. It wraps itself around you, like the red lizard, and never stops its invasive chatter. That chatter finds its way into your thoughts, how you see others, and how you see yourself. It tempts and prods and accuses and shames without ceasing, even subconsciously, but it makes you feel as if you can't live without it. Jay Stringer explains this complexity:

> In my view, our self-contempt is not a by-product of unwanted sexual behavior; it is the very aim of it. Through this lens, unwanted sexual behavior is not primarily an attempt to remedy or self-soothe the pain of a wounded child. It is attempting to reenact the formative stories of trauma, abuse, and shame that convinced us we were unwanted to begin with. In other words, we are not addicted primarily to sex or even a disordered intimacy; instead, we are bonded to feelings of shame and judgment. In this way, unwanted sexual behavior is not seeking medication but rather a familiar poison to deaden our imagination that something could change for the better.[3]

The bondage to shame and judgment Stringer articulates so well is the narrative we find illustrated by Lewis through the red lizard; our shame is the primary reason for keeping our sin around, *not* vice versa. When shame becomes embedded in our identity, we look for actions that will reinforce it. We wonder, however crazy it may sound, who we'll be if we let go of our sin, and that uncertainty makes it feel safer to just remain where we stand.

The angel's continual prodding in *The Great Divorce* is a beautiful portrayal of the gentle but firm invitation of God when it comes to our habitual sin. At one point, the ghost tries to opt for a "gradual process" of letting the lizard die:

> "Honestly, I don't think there's the slightest necessity for that. I'm sure I shall be able to keep it in order now. I think the gradual process would be far better than killing it."
>
> "The gradual process is of no use at all."
>
> "Don't you think so? Well, I'll think over what you've said very carefully. I honestly will. In fact I'd let

you kill it now, but as a matter of fact I'm not feeling
frightfully well today. It would be silly to do it now.
I'd need to be in good health for the operation. Some
other day, perhaps."

"There is no other day. All days are present now."[4]

Just as the angel responds to the ghost's fear and cowardice, "the
gradual process is of no use at all." While recovery is a process we
commit to long term, making excuses for our sin has to die, and
die as quickly as possible. There's a massive difference between
practicing endurance and compassion with ourselves during the
process of healing and making excuses to keep our sinful and
shame-reinforcing behavior around. The invitation of God is to
surrender, and surrender now—"there is no other day." The next
part of the ghost's dialogue with the angel shows how deep our
attachment to our sin can go:

"I cannot kill it against your will. It is impossible. Have
I your permission?"

The Angel's hands were almost closed on the
Lizard, but not quite. Then the Lizard began chattering
to the Ghost so loud that even I could hear what it
was saying. "Be careful," it said. "He can do what he
says. He can kill me. One fatal word from you and he
will! Then you'll be without me for ever and ever. It's
not natural. How could you live? You'd be only a sort
of ghost, not a real man as you are now. He doesn't
understand. He's only a cold, bloodless abstract thing.
It may be natural for him, but it isn't for us. Yes, yes. I
know there are no real pleasures now, only dreams. But
aren't they better than nothing? And I'll be so good. I
admit I've sometimes gone too far in the past, but I
promise I won't do it again. I'll give you nothing but
really nice dreams—all sweet and fresh and almost
innocent. You might say, quite innocent . . ."

"Have I your permission?" said the Angel to the
Ghost.

"I know it will kill me."

> "It won't. But supposing it did?"
>
> "You're right. It would be better to be dead than to live with this creature."
>
> "Then I may?"
>
> "Damn and blast you! Go on can't you? Get it over. Do what you like," bellowed the Ghost: but ended, whimpering, "God help me. God help me." Next moment the Ghost gave a scream of agony such as I never heard on Earth. The Burning One closed his crimson grip on the reptile: twisted it, while it bit and writhed, and then flung it, broken backed, on the turf. "Ow! That's done for me," gasped the Ghost, reeling backwards.[5]

The evolution of the lizard's conversation with the ghost is key here. As it becomes more and more aware that its life is threatened, the lizard becomes louder and more insistent. The ghost feels the intense struggle between the chatter of the lizard, who promises he'll be "almost innocent"; his own exhaustion; and the angel's continued gentle beckoning.

I felt that imperative invitation while sharing the scene from the book with my friend, but even more so as I walked into a night of adoration at a healing retreat on my campus a couple of weeks later. I had the scene in the back of my mind, and it felt like the ghost making excuses for why today couldn't be the day, why I wasn't ready, why getting rid of my lizard would kill me. I wanted it to be me who could get rid of it, not God. I felt the same promises of the red lizard—that it would calm down, be "almost innocent," as long as I didn't try to give it up. But the exhaustion felt so heavy and so real that I could no longer ignore it.

My roommate and I had ditched the rest of the retreat (nineteen-year-old me preferred the drive-through option to the three-course meal), but we walked in early to adoration. There was a panel of speakers finishing up a Q&A session, and almost immediately after we walked in and stood in the very back, the microphone was handed to one of the speakers who said, "There's a scene in C. S. Lewis's *The Great Divorce* about a ghost with a red lizard around his shoulders . . ." I have no memory of what question the speaker was answering; all I remember is feeling *seen* where I stood. God's invitation rang loud and clear in my heart once again: "You're not leaving this room until we deal with this."

And so we did.

I knelt and prayed as the Eucharist was exposed, and we were led through a guided meditation about wearing our sin like a garment and taking it to the Father's house where we could allow him to embrace us and clothe us anew. I wept—the good, cleansing, snot-filled kind of weeping—as I finally allowed my exhaustion to open my hands to the Lord and the freedom he'd been offering all along. I allowed myself to tell him that I was a pornography addict and I was *so tired of myself*, but that finally I believed him—I believed he could help me be free and that he *wanted* to help me, that he was the only one who could. I wore the hours spent with pornography, lust, and shame as my dirty garment, and I let myself be embraced by a loving Father who showed me how welcome I still was, despite what I believed about myself. I didn't need to find the way out—he was offering it.

Later on in adoration, we had the opportunity to participate in a practice called individual exposition, where you kneel and have the chance for the monstrance to be directly in front of you. It's an incredibly moving and overwhelming experience, particularly in settings focused on healing like this. I knelt in the line, shoulder to shoulder with peers and classmates, and waited for my turn. As the monstrance was moved down the line, I kept my eyes fixed on the crucifix in front of us as tears kept streaming down my cheeks. I remember saying in my heart over and over, "Can I really be done, Lord? Do I really get to be done?"

As the monstrance passed in front of me and it was my turn to be literally face-to-face with Jesus, all I heard was "It is finished." I could barely lift my head.

My struggle with pornography didn't end that night; it would be several more months until I entered long-term sobriety. But I felt that red lizard ripped from my shoulders that night; the bondage with shame and my own sin to repeatedly feed its narrative felt broken. I had spent an entire evening allowing my exhaustion to turn into a recognition of what I've done and what's been done for me, and because of finally accepting that reality, my struggle with sexual sin would never have the same power again.

Grace and Slowness

One of my favorite quotes is "Above all, trust in the slow work of God."[6] There's a tendency among faith-based communities, when they speak about addiction, to say that all it takes *is* the moment of surrender I've laid out above in order to be free of addictive behaviors. It's important to distinguish between surrender coupled with the reception of grace to break an agreement with sin and shame and the end of the sinful behavior itself. The latter, during our earthly walk, will never fully end. What surrender *doesn't* do is put an instant stop to our behavior. Instead, what it *does* do is give us the hope necessary to move forward and the trust that we're loved even as we explore the complexity of what got us into our unwanted behavior in the first place. Recall that second step in the twelve-step recovery model: surrendering to a higher Power that can restore you. When we allow our exhaustion to transform into surrender, we turn our focus away from our own willpower, white-knuckling, and grasping at control to entrusting the hardest work to the grace of God.

We can't "pray addiction away," but we can find the end of trying to do it on our own in our prayer. We can hit the wall of our own willpower in prayer. We can encounter the transformative love of Christ in prayer. All of these things don't often mean instant change; instead, they're catalysts for the kind of change that lasts. No matter how slow the process may be, God makes sure that it's thorough. Surrender allows us to see his loving, guiding hand in the process of our healing as we move forward.

I see that moment of surrender in adoration not as the "end" of my struggle with pornography but rather as the beginning of a beautiful journey of reflection, hope, and transformation in the love of Jesus. It was the beginning of me *learning to learn* about and love my story, instead of trying to find my own answers in control—that is, refusing to listen to the manipulative chatter of the red lizard and instead listening to the tender invitation of God.

5
RADICAL HONESTY

Our whole existence depends upon truth.
–Romano Guardini

A friend reached out to me recently asking if I had heard of the concept of "radical honesty." A popular practice among recovering drug and alcohol addicts, radical honesty is a recommended counterattack to the spirit of dishonesty and deception that addiction almost always creates. I had indeed heard of it, and I try to practice it, but the concept almost makes me want to smirk when it comes to women and sexual sin. How can we expect women to be radically honest about a struggle that's barely acknowledged to begin with?

My initial reaction to the concept is just a sign of my own lack of knowledge about its power and how, once honesty begins (as anyone in recovery from any type of addiction knows), it's pretty hard to stop—in the best of ways.

The Value of Disclosure

I've joked that talking about my job is my "party trick." It's pretty fun to be at your average, run-of-the-mill young adult social, holding a beer, and when someone asks "What do you do?" you get to say, "I help women recover from sexual addiction. What do you do?" Whether their answer is that they're an accountant, a nurse, or a unicyclist, I almost always have the conversation-starting career—or the career that makes people back away from me *slowly*.

I'm only half joking. People's reactions to the work I do can vary from being affirming to asking a lot of questions and to not knowing how to react at all—and I can't blame them. Sex is an uncomfortable topic, so naturally sexual addiction is even *more* uncomfortable. This is where radical honesty doesn't just help your integrity (which we'll get to in a moment) but also helps you be prepared for the multitude of reactions you're going to get when you *do* disclose. The fact that I'm incredibly public, for the sake of my work, about my own struggle with sexual sin can either be something that petrifies me into becoming a recluse or frees me, giving me the confidence I need to receive people exactly where they are. I can either be put off when someone wants to talk to me about porn addiction at that party or on the sidewalk after Mass or I can recognize that honesty is doing its work, opening the door to others and freeing me from the fear of being "found out" that so many addicts, including those in recovery, suffer from.

Hiding Creates Lying

It's a normal part of a young child's development to learn to lie. I nannied a four-year-old girl for a few months recently, and I saw her hitting this stage full force: our battle was usually over whether or not she had washed her hands in the bathroom. She didn't lie to be malicious; she did it because she's learning the value of the truth, whether it can be bent, and what the consequences are if it is.

When you're struggling with an addiction to any behavior or substance, you almost hit this stage of development all over again. When you have a sin that feels worth hiding—not just worth hiding but *imperative* to hide—the questions come up: *What is truth? What value does it actually have? And what are the consequences if I bend it, even just by omission? Even just a little?*

The consequence of not living in the truth is made clear in scripture. John 8:32 says, "You will know the truth, and the truth will set you free." Likewise, Jesus calls himself "the way and the *truth* and the life" (Jn 14:6, emphasis added). To distance ourselves or hide from the truth is to distance ourselves or hide from Christ, full stop. If we want to experience the fullness of his life, we have to be willing to experience the fullness of the truth. Sin has caused us to hide ourselves at the cost of communion with God, since the beginning. If we look again to Genesis, after Adam and Eve had sinned and "knew that they were naked," they first hid their own bodies (3:7). Immediately there's a recognition of the options that sin leaves us: expose ourselves in shame or hide behind the fig leaves and maintain a shred of dignity, even if it means we can never have true communion again.

The hiding doesn't stop there. Genesis then says, "When they heard the sound of the LORD God walking about in the garden at the breezy time of the day, the man and his wife hid themselves from the LORD God among the trees of the garden. The LORD God then called to the man and asked him: Where are you? He answered, 'I heard you in the garden; but I was afraid, because I was naked, so I hid'" (Gn 3:8–10). The "sound of the LORD God walking about" was the next layer of Adam and Eve being reminded that their options were to reveal imperfection and betrayal or cover themselves even further. The shame pushed them even deeper into hiding. God's question pricks at the places of our hearts and lives where we know we're hiding in the bushes right along with our first parents: *"Where are you?"*

Addictions thrive when we hide. Shame reinforces our belief that we're not worth knowing, being seen, being loved—pick your poison—and convinces us that the only way to survive is to be alone, to hide. Lying seemingly protects us from the pain of possible rejection that we could receive from others if they knew of our behaviors, but it's also a self-fulfilling prophecy: we end up experiencing rejection in our lying and hiding anyway. We're just rejecting ourselves, over and over again, before anyone else has the chance to do it. When I was in my addictive cycle, hiding had a very obvious role. I would typically only watch porn alone and often after I had gone to hide in my room after experiencing a difficult day at school or a conflict with someone I loved. My little sister recently shared with me that she vividly remembers me quickly closing my computer or putting my phone down the moment she walked into the room we shared—hiding at work.

It's hard to learn to unhide and tell the truth because it becomes a lifestyle. Next to pornography, lying was perhaps the sin I struggled with the most in my teenage years. Lying—whether in the form of outright lying, embellishing details, or omitting the truth when it was risky—bled into most aspects of my life, and it even got me into *massive* trouble at school one year. I lost friendships over a mountain of lies I had built up. It wasn't that I *wanted* to lie; it was that I had to keep lying to keep hiding, and I wasn't willing to stop hiding yet.

Though I've put several years of distance between myself and those years of deep hiding and lying, and the divorce from reality they created, occasionally the habits I built will still show up. When we were dating, my husband gently pointed out to me that if I used my phone in front of him, I always tilted it away from him, hiding whatever was on the screen even if it was just my texts or GPS. I winced and quickly made the connection for him. I had gotten used to hiding my screens from people for years, and clearly something in me still felt the need to, despite the fact that I wasn't viewing anything objectionable or sinful anymore.

Honesty and Freedom

Radical honesty is the most surefire way to unlearn the pattern of hiding and lying and even the habits that remain once the pattern itself is broken. It feels painfully embarrassing and even dangerous at first, but you quickly see the freedom that only honesty can provide. The psychiatrist Anna Lembke, in her book *Dopamine Nation*, describes radical honesty and why it's beneficial for *everyone*, not just those in recovery:

> Radical honesty—telling the truth about things large and small, especially when doing so exposes our foibles and entails consequences—is essential not just to recovery from addiction but for all of us trying to live a more balanced life in our reward-saturated ecosystem. It works on many levels.
>
> First, radical honesty promotes awareness of our actions. Second, it fosters intimate human connections. Third, it leads to a truthful autobiography, which holds us accountable not just to our present but also to our future selves. Further, telling the truth is contagious, and might even prevent the development of future addiction.[1]

Lembke's definition and summary of the effectiveness of radical honesty can easily be deepened from a secular ethic to a Catholic one. Radical honesty helps us thoroughly examine our consciences and properly experience contrition and repentance. It creates unity between the self, God, and others—the unity we crave—and it holds us in right relationship with reality. And, like Lembke says, telling the truth is truly contagious, not just because of the act of telling the truth itself but also because of the freedom we experience in Christ when we do.

I shared about my struggle in recovery privately multiple times. It became almost commonplace, to the point that I can't recall many pivotal moments from those individual disclosures. I know the first few were difficult; the closer the person was to me, the more difficult the disclosure was. However, I was blessed *by* the commonplace feeling of the conversation. Sometimes friends and others said "Me too" in response, or thanked me for telling them—either way, the conversation ended and nothing changed for the worse, only for the better.

My first public disclosure, referenced in the introduction, was also a truly blessed experience. Holding a sign in front of me with my sin written clearly upon it—"Chained by an addiction to pornography"—in front of hundreds of campers, staff, and friends was one of the most intimidating moments of my life. I got to flip that sign over and place the focus on Jesus, letting the crowd know the freedom he had brought me in the previous year and how far I'd come from the girl who felt as if she was living a double life on her college campus. The intimidation quickly turned into a feeling of deep gratitude, and the encouragement of others only increased that feeling.

I cried some incredibly liberating tears that day, and I believe it was the day I was bitten by the "honesty bug" or experienced the contagiousness of radical honesty that Lembke described above. I felt the freedom that honesty could bring—not just to me but to women in particular—and I wanted that freedom to be at the core of my life and testimony. The opportunity arose on my campus the following fall, in my junior year, to speak at a women's retreat. I had been feeling a pull from the Holy Spirit to begin sharing my story of pornography addiction with more women, and a friend asked if I would speak at a retreat she was organizing. The words tumbled out of my mouth before I realized how crazy it might sound: "Sure, can I talk about porn?"

To my friend's credit, she was hardly taken aback. "Absolutely, you can," she said.

Getting through the preparation for that retreat was a painful experience since it was my first time sharing an extended version of my story more publicly. I broke down sobbing in my first run-through of my talk, and I remember stepping out of the room to hyperventilate for a minute before actually giving it at the retreat. After that first small experience, I've never sobbed or hyperventilated again, because the fruit of honesty was so apparent—in myself and in others. That talk led to others, and by my senior year of college, all of my close friends and many of my peers knew that pornography addiction was part of my story because it was a large part of my ministry work on campus. The thought had scared me initially, but the feeling of integration that came from owning my story—the good and bad—gave me an unshakable sense of freedom. Rejection from others didn't hurt nearly as much when I had ceased to reject myself. When people back away from me slowly (again, half kidding) or don't know what to say in response to my story or work, I know that their response is far more about them than it is about me. Perhaps there's something in their own story that they haven't stopped hiding yet, and I can relate. When we stop the cycle of shame, hiding, lying, and rejecting ourselves right back into that cycle, the reactions of others are left to be exactly what they are: reactions from flawed, dignified human beings who are carrying their own cross and can only react based on their own conglomeration of experiences, emotions, and convictions.

Honesty and Lasting Recovery

People regularly ask me if it bothers me that others know about my journey with addiction or if it bothers my husband and those close to me. I've perpetually found that I'm usually only bothered by people's perceptions of my story or the authority that they think it gives them to speak into my life. I've had relative strangers try to pry deeper into my recovery or even tell me that the worst is yet to come. (Encouraging, right?) But this, once again, is more about them than me. I've continued to find a deep liberation in sharing my story, even in an increasingly public manner, and I've seen the same liberation in the lives of many addicts. They also find the same detachment from any embarrassment or fear that might convince them to stay silent, recognizing it as a close relative of the shame they've actively worked to be free from. The same goes for those close to a recovering addict who is discovering the power of honesty; when we love someone, what we ultimately desire is their freedom. When loved ones see increased freedom through honesty in the life of the person they love in recovery, they're not apt to be thinking of themselves or any effects that honesty might have on their personal lives.

Honesty can certainly take a turn for the vicious, as all of our actions can, even when we're aspiring for goodness. Dr. Lembke, in her treatment of radical honesty, points out that telling the truth and the bonding it can often create in our relationships initiates a release of dopamine, or the "pleasure hormone" (the same one released in droves by sexual compulsions). As she says, "Any behavior that leads to an increase in dopamine has the potential to be exploited."[2] We can exploit our honesty when we use our stories to manipulate others, or make it about selfish gratification rather than the liberation that comes from telling the truth and giving others space to do the same. In examining our desire to share, it's always important to check our motivations for one of these hallmarks of selfishness and manipulation creeping in; it can do incredible damage to our long-term freedom.

Further, honesty is an ongoing way to take responsibility for your actions. Each time I tell my story, I have the opportunity to both have compassion for my woundedness and take responsibility for the ways I sought my satisfaction and answers in the wrong places. Sharing about addiction requires you to look at the moments you fell to sin, as we say in the Penitential Act, "in what you have done, and in what you have failed to do." When sharing, you can't leave out the ways you avoided pursuing tools that would help free you, shrugged off accountability, or lied to cover up your trail. You have to be willing to be honest about it *all*, not just the parts that garner sympathy and inspire awe. To truly motivate those who might be struggling around you, they need to be able to see a piece of their own story in yours, including all the ups and downs inherent to *every* human story, whether addiction is involved or not.

Disclosing Well

If you're a woman currently struggling with sexual sin and addiction, you may be reading this and wondering exactly *how* to go about being honest. Initially, disclosure of your addiction or compulsive behavior needs to occur. Radical honesty is a lifestyle that comes about afterward.

Disclosure can be separated into two categories: public and private. Private disclosure is when you have control over who the recipients are, whether that's a one-on-one coffee date with a friend or a twelve-step meeting. Private disclosures are typically understood to be confidential. A public disclosure is when you don't necessarily have control over who is in the audience and who might find out as a result of that disclosure. First of all, public disclosure is by no means a requirement for recovery, and it's certainly not for everyone. I don't recommend putting it all out there in an Instagram post unless you feel specifically called to do so and can see obvious fruits for doing so. Again, public disclosure should be more about the people listening than about you—not a way to "get it over with" or garner attention. Private disclosure, however, is essentially necessary to make a healthy recovery, even if it's to just a few people who can help you along your journey.

Talking privately with a trusted friend or family member is the best way to begin being honest about your struggle. Telling my best friend in high school was a much simpler experience than I imagined it would be, and she embraced the conversation with love and acceptance, just as she would if I had told her about any other sin or habit in my life that was harming my relationship with God. When it comes to telling that first person or few people, you hopefully don't have to look too hard; you already know who you can trust, because I hope they've already shown you. Think of whose wisdom you turn to when dealing with difficulties or whose advice you lean on when looking for a solution to something big or small. Whom do you look to as an example of virtue? Whose prayer life do you admire and trust? Whose ability to keep things private and confidential do you trust? As you ask yourself these questions, perhaps a few people come to mind—maybe it's a friend, a spiritual director or therapist, or a family member. Whoever they are, reach out and as soon as possible.

I recommend initiating these conversations without too much drama or pressure. Instead, you can simply say, "I have something that's been really weighing on my heart, and I'd like to ask for your help and prayers"; or "I have a sin that I've been really struggling to kick. Could I talk about it with you?" There's a way to prepare someone for a serious conversation without adding an unnecessary intensity to it. I've had the privilege of being on both sides of a disclosure conversation, both in ministry and as a friend. The fruit of vulnerability—especially in the context of friendship—is twofold: it frees you, as the addict, by bringing you out of isolation; and it gives your friend or loved one the opportunity to love you, show you mercy, and come alongside you in a way they haven't before. Disclosure can be something that strengthens relationships, not hurts them.

Disclosure in Romantic Relationships

Perhaps one of the most frequent questions I get is *when* and *how* to tell a significant other that you're struggling with pornography, masturbation, or another sexual sin—or have them in your history. There is no set formula for telling someone you're in a relationship with; each relationship is unique and has different needs. However, despite the differences from relationship to relationship, I recommend being honest as soon as possible, especially if you anticipate that your history or current struggle will make it difficult to practice chastity in a relationship.

There's no way around it—it's terrifying to imagine telling a man you're beginning to fall for about something as taboo as a pornography or masturbation addiction. Remember, in those moments where it feels terrifying, that you are only in charge of yourself, not how he reacts. Additionally, it's crucial to remember that you do not have to tell him *everything* in one sitting. In fact, it would probably be unhealthy if you did. Your story, including this part of it, deserves to unfold in front of someone as your relationship does. You do not owe a man you're dating a detailed account of your sexual sin.

What *is* helpful to disclose is *what* your struggle is or was (pornography, masturbation, fantasizing, sexual behavior in relationships, etc.), whether the struggle is still present, and if it is, what you're doing to work toward recovery or maintain recovery, such as membership in a support group, therapy, an accountability partner, or filtering software. What *isn't* helpful is graphic details of these behaviors or asking your new significant other to keep you accountable. It's important to have your own game plan that they can be clued in on, but especially at the beginning of a relationship, it's not helpful for them to be heavily involved in your recovery. It can be healthy, as your relationship progresses, for your boyfriend to check in on your progress or be aware if you're experiencing a relapse. Once again, the gritty details of these things should be reserved for spiritual direction, support groups, therapy, or an accountability partner and close friends.

If you're engaged, it can be a good time to start discussing how addiction has shaped your understanding of sexuality and sex more in-depth. Sharing concerns, fears, or uncertainties about your sexual relationship in your upcoming marriage—while still guarding the conversation with prudence to make sure it's productive and fruitful, not pleasurable or inducing temptation—can not only prepare you for the possibility of difficulties but also help you deepen your love and compassion for one another. Chances are, the person you're marrying will have his own set of uncertainties and fears about sex within a marriage—and his own history to reconcile with. After all, he's human too.

In marriage, the need for disclosure and honesty becomes abundantly necessary. Because of the sacredness of marriage vows, struggling with sexual sin and addiction within a marriage becomes an affront to those vows, not just damaging to a romantic relationship. Disclosing to a spouse, or habits being discovered by a spouse, can be incredibly painful and traumatic for both of you, in different ways. If you are currently struggling with a sexual behavior that violates your marriage vows, it's important to be honest with your spouse as soon as possible. Sometimes it's best to seek the help of a professional—whether that's a therapist, priest, or pastoral authority you trust—when disclosing the details of addiction to your husband. Someone who is experienced in these kinds of disclosures can help guide the conversation and make space for both your story and your spouse's reaction.

When disclosing to anyone, especially in a romantic context of any level of commitment, it's crucial to allow your partner to have their own reaction. Trying to control their reaction—whether it's confusion, pain, or silence—almost always ends up damaging their trust, when that's the most important thing to create in disclosure conversations. If you can, express that you understand this information might be a lot for them to take in and that you want them to process it in the healthiest way possible for them. There are plenty of ways to do this without being self-deprecating to yourself or your story, or putting words in your partner's mouth. Establishing or deepening trust, even when you're speaking about something incredibly difficult, embarrassing, and painful, comes down to creating room for the other person to feel safe to be themselves, and this is done primarily through how you allow them to react and you receiving that reaction lovingly.

Spiritual writer Henri Nouwen speaks of vulnerability in our relationships creating community (and he even speaks to the value of it over public disclosure). Referring to our life as our "cup," he articulates why private disclosure of our inner life, including sins and addictions, is fundamental for our embracing the fullness life has to offer:

> I am not suggesting that everyone we know or meet should hear about what is in our cup. To the contrary, it would be tactless, unwise, and even dangerous to expose our innermost being to people who cannot offer us safety and trust. That does not create community; it only causes mutual embarrassment and deepens our shame and guilt. But I do suggest we need loving and caring friends with whom we can speak from the depth of our heart. Such friends take away the paralysis that

secrecy creates. They can offer us a safe and sacred place, where we can express our deepest sorrows and joys, and they can confront us in love, challenging us to a greater spiritual maturity. We might object by saying, "I do not have such trustworthy friends, and I wouldn't know how to find them." But this objection comes from our fear of drinking the cup that Jesus asks us to drink.[3]

Nouwen's words have a deeply convicting tone when read in light of disclosure. For him, having a few trusted people that we can reveal our "deepest sorrows and joys" to is necessary not just for recovery but also for following God's call for our very *life*.

Public disclosure, as Nouwen points out, isn't what creates community; vulnerability and trust in friendship, engaged in bravely and repeatedly on an ever-deepening level, does. My public testimony is not what has offered me the most healing; my private conversations about my journey with those who love me have been. The story I tell publicly is only the tip of the iceberg. The deeper story, as with all of us, should remain sacred and entrusted to those who love us the most.

Embodying Honesty

In order for the truth to actually set us free, radical honesty needs to become a lifestyle, just as lying often does in addiction. Lying, even little lies, can slowly build up over time and literally create the feeling of a different reality, which leads to us dissociating from God, others, ourselves, and the life he's given us. Taking intentional steps forward in honesty in *all* areas, not just disclosing addiction or sexual sin, is what gets us back in touch with reality as it *is*, not as we create it to be for our own protection.

If you recognize that lying is a pattern in your life—or even if you don't—set a goal of not lying for one day. Don't embellish stories. Don't tell fibs or white lies about why you were late to class or work, or why you can't hang out with so-and-so this weekend. Tell the truth, even if it hurts. This doesn't mean you unearth your deepest, darkest secrets in a day. It just means beginning the habit of letting the truth reign in your daily life, along with the peace only living in reality can bring.

Especially after a long period of hiding, being honest about *everything*, including a struggle with sexual sin and addiction, feels like a massive breath of fresh air. Yes, it can be terrifying in the moment to disclose—especially when, as I mentioned earlier, so few women speak up to begin with. But just think: maybe your story, and the small way you tell it today, isn't just a breath of fresh air for you; it may be the motivation and permission for someone else to come out of hiding and live in the freedom of truth, too.

6
RECOVERING RELATIONSHIP

The soul of woman must be expansive and
open to all human beings, it must be quiet so
that no small weak flame will be extinguished
by stormy winds; warm so as not to benumb
fragile buds . . . empty of itself, in order that
extraneous life may have room in it; finally,
mistress of itself and also of its body, so that
the entire person is readily at the disposal of
every call.

–St. Edith Stein

Love is my identity . . . Love is my name.
–Thomas Merton

Early on in my recovery, I was introduced to Young Life, the
ministry that would take me to the camp where I would first share
about my addiction publicly. Young Life is a nondenominational
Christian youth ministry that's been operating since 1941 (they
like to use the motto "Serving up fun since 1941"), and it
powerfully brings together Christians of all different traditions

and denominations under the sole pretense of loving Jesus and living the Gospel. In the area surrounding my college, Young Life particularly reached teenagers from immigrant families, most from Haiti and many of them facing poverty and other challenges.

I stepped into Young Life somewhat hesitant, both as a newcomer to the organization as a whole and to my college campus, but I very quickly fell in love with the girls I came to serve. And in the years since, I can see that loving them solidified a massive part of my healing and recovery. Without them and the depth of friendship I was surrounded by in my college years, I doubt my recovery would have lasted into the long term.

Lust and Selfishness

Similar to the habit of lying, lust makes a habit of selfishness. St. Thomas Aquinas refers to lust causing a "blindness of mind,"[1] which not only causes the "lack of filter" that's becoming steadily more and more socially acceptable but also obscures you to the needs, feelings, and good of others. We may think that our sexual behaviors are affecting only one sphere of our life and can be kept to ourselves, but the habit of prioritizing pleasure or release over the good of our own spiritual and physical well-being bleeds into prioritizing it everywhere else, over *everything* and *everyone* else. This selfishness is conflicting and heartbreaking, and often goes against our outward commitments. Many of the married women I work with, in particular, are distraught over their treatment of their husbands beyond just their sexual relationships. They say similar things: "He's been so faithful and so sacrificial—why can't I just be that way back?" or "No matter how hard I try, I just can't think about him and be present to him . . . my mind is constantly wandering to all my fantasies."

Our selfishness in addiction isn't just a moral issue; it's also a neurological one. The well-known phrase "What fires together, wires together" applies here: addiction and compulsion wire together not just different acts but also emotions, events, times of day, and locations with pleasure, making each day an endless opportunity to choose yourself, whether you like it or not. Recovery, on both a moral and a mental level, requires us to begin rewiring ourselves toward choosing others—and meaningful relationships with them—over ourselves and whatever might be easiest or pleasurable in the moment.

Turning Outward

The young man who motivated me to reach a new level of recovery and healing by quitting pornography for good asked to end our relationship after a few months, sending my nineteen-year-old self into a bit of a tailspin. I had thought that a restoration of love, romance, and affection would come from that relationship, but the breakup ended up providing the healing I actually needed. He asked if we could remain friends, a request that I could hardly refuse as he was in a period of deep suffering within his family. I had little to no desire to be friends, but I said yes anyway.

That yes had effects I could never have predicted. Saying no to what I wanted—a relationship—and "yes" to what he was asking for and needed—a faithful friend—began that process of rewiring. Loving this person in front of me actually, at the end of the day, had nothing to do with me. If I truly wanted to love, I needed to lay down my own ease, pleasure, and feelings and instead prioritize his good, as long as it didn't conflict with what was emotionally healthy for me. It wasn't that I didn't know how to do this at all but rather that when I reflect, I can see the threads of selfishness woven through many of my relationships with friends and family throughout my teenage years and even into college. I had thought that rewiring was simply about recovering a holy understanding of romance, but that was the tip of the iceberg. It was about recovering a prioritization of charity and sacrifice, the ability to lay down my life for a friend, as Jesus asks of us.

This new pain of sacrifice was excruciating to my recovering heart, but it broke me wide open. It felt like stretching your arms wide after waking up, or the soreness after doing something physically challenging—it hurt, but I could feel the worth and purpose in the pain itself. Pornography, lust, and fantasizing had made my heart and mind feel as if they were atrophying; heartbreak made them feel, for the first time in a long time, that they were throbbing with pain but *alive.*

Dr. Anna Lembke speaks about the relationship, on a physiological level, between pleasure and pain. In her thought, the scale of pleasure and pain that keeps us in balance, when tipped too far toward pleasure repeatedly, needs to be counteracted by "pressing the pain side."[2] She cites situations of drug addicts who undergo daily ice baths to reset their dopamine receptors—perhaps heartbreak and sacrifice are an "ice bath" for lust. Encountering the pain of love—whether romantic, familial, or in friendship—is a wake-up call to the lust's emptiness. C. S. Lewis, in *The Four Loves*, articulates in supernatural tones what Lembke is saying on the natural level:

> I believe that the most lawless and inordinate loves
> are less contrary to God's will than a self-invited and
> self-protective lovelessness. It is like hiding the talent
> in a napkin and for much the same reason. "I knew
> thee that thou wert a hard man." Christ did not teach
> and suffer that we might become, even in the natural
> loves, more careful of our own happiness. If a man is
> not uncalculating towards the earthly beloveds whom
> he has seen, he is none the more likely to be so towards
> God whom he has not. We shall draw nearer to God,
> not by trying to avoid the sufferings inherent in all
> loves, but by accepting them and offering them to Him;
> throwing away all defensive armour. If our hearts need
> to be broken, and if He chooses this as the way in which
> they should break, so be it.[3]

Pornography, masturbation, and other sexual sins—for whatever reason one originally seeks them—are breeders of the "self-protective lovelessness" that Lewis describes above. When what

I thought would make me happy was no longer available, I had to undergo the process of confronting not just the pain of losing what I thought I wanted but also the pain of learning that what I want—when it comes to deeply, charitably loving others—does not take priority in the first place. My heart *did* need to be broken, and I'm profoundly grateful for the way that God chose. It would truly take a process of learning this, and it's a lesson I still desperately need to keep learning—that true love, the love we crave, demands that we lay ourselves down. But, as our Lord promises in scripture, in losing our life we truly find it.

My heart, in that opportune time of being broken wide open, was able to welcome those dear teenagers at Young Life whom God entrusted to my care that year, in a way I don't think I would've been able to before. I would drive an hour one way just to be at a high school lunch with them to lead a devotional or give a talk, or just to hang out with them and build a discipleship relationship with them. Several people asked why I gave the time and money to do this several times a week as a volunteer, with a full load of college classes, and I couldn't totally explain my drive and dedication at the time. I knew they needed me, in a way, but deep down I also knew that *I* needed *them.*

There's something incredibly convicting about knowing others are watching you, especially if those others are younger and easily influenced. It wasn't that these teens knew anything about my addiction at the time but rather that my spiritual and emotional health mattered to them. If I wasn't receiving healing and striving for virtue, I couldn't offer them anything—and the last thing I wanted was for them to be drawing from an empty well. Beyond the conviction of being an example, having the opportunity to love, serve, and sacrifice for them, in a way that didn't expect or demand return, tipped the scale for me. Over time, temptations became less and less, because love was taking up more and more room.

Relational Healing

There are plenty of psychological reasons why support groups work for recovering addicts. Groups like Alcoholics Anonymous have seen countless people enter recovery and turn their lives around. When I lead support groups for women, I see this principle of recovering in relationships be the crux of the reordering of their love. Many women think that it's in a romantic relationship or future marriage that they'll find closure and healing from their sexual sin—more on that later—but I've seen, time and time again personally and professionally, that the Lord begins with healing us in sisterhood.

I was leading a virtual group several months ago with a fairly quiet group—it was their first meeting, and their nerves made for a not-so-chatty conversation with lots of pauses. I've seen many meetings go this way. At the very end, I asked, "Are there any questions or anything that anyone would like to add before we wrap up?" One woman, who had her Zoom camera and microphone switched off during the whole meeting, quickly switched on her microphone and said, "I just wanted to say one thing: I feel hope now. That's all."

My heart swelled at her words. I've seen it work in every group I've been a part of. There's something about women who struggle with sexual addictions and compulsions simply seeing and hearing one another that sparks hope. The natural inclination we have toward relationships with others—intuition, the ability to create space for people in our hearts and minds in a way that's unique to women—is not lost in recovery. That natural giftedness, though individually expressed in radically different ways, is still there, and it quickly rises to the surface. I've seen women weep compassionately at one another's stories, and weep at the freedom of being able to share their own in community, when they hardly know each other. They link arms to heal together, and man, do they do it fast. Women in support groups experience a similar thing to what a breakup and ministry provided for me in my first years of recovery—the pain of being vulnerable, showing up for others and investing in their good, and recognizing that your recovery matters not just to you but also to those around you, whether they know about it or not.

In the case of several women I've had the joy of walking with to healing, the simple act of joining a group is enough to help them achieve a lasting period of sobriety and sometimes even long-term recovery. For some, it's the ability to share and see a greater purpose for their pain and regret. For others, it's receiving the stories of others. For some, it's the motivation to pray and invest in the other group members' recovery even more so than their own. Whatever the reason, the sobriety comes from being filled by a new love, one that demands more of them, and motivates them to leave the cheap filler of lust behind, even if just for a longer period of time than they were able to before.

Recovering All the Loves

C. S. Lewis, in *The Four Loves*, speaks of love in four categories (in accordance with the four Greek words for love): affection (*storge*), friendship (*philia*), romance (*eros*), and charity (*agape*). Recovering true relationship and communion, for any person in recovery, means rehabilitating *all* four of the loves, not just romance. Pornography, masturbation, and sexual sin—and the selfishness they bring when engaged in habitually—damage the ability to love in general, not just in sexual and romantic relationships. Our selfishness and compulsions affect our ability to prioritize family, friends, and even workplace productivity or camaraderie. In the small-group model my ministry team and I have developed for the women who come to us for support, we devote time to studying and reflecting on all four loves and how to recover them.

Recovering Affection

Described by Lewis as "the humblest love," affection is perhaps also the most overlooked or underrated. It's easily mistaken as just an expression of other loves—which it can certainly participate with—rather than being understood as a love all its own. Affectionate love is present in our daily relationships, with people who are or aren't close to us, whether it's family, friends, a spouse, children, coworkers, or acquaintances. It's a comforting, familiar sort of love that, as Lewis writes, "opens our eyes to goodness we could not have seen, or should not have appreciated without it."[4]

Sexual compulsions and addictions destroy our affection by slowly chipping away at our ability to experience the appreciative, unassuming, lighthearted love that affection offers. When people become objects for our enjoyment rather than brothers and sisters in Christ, we are unable to see and delight in their inherent goodness. Affection is a love that depends on us doing such. As Lewis says, "Affection can love the unattractive: God and His saints love the unlovable. Affection 'does not expect too much,' turns a blind eye to faults, revives easily after quarrels."[5] When people become valuable only insofar as they are attractive to us—whether in an exterior or an interior way—we lose the ability to be affectionate, no matter how close we may be to them.

Rehabilitating affection, in my experience, doesn't come in physical expression—what we may think of when we think of "affection"—but rather in gratitude. Gratitude has a way of restoring our sight to take in what things actually *are* rather than simply how we perceive them. This is why St. Paul exhorts us to "in all circumstances give thanks" (1 Thes 5:18); in giving thanks, our vision becomes subject to God's, allowing his vision of our circumstances to shape how we perceive them.[6] When we habituate ourselves to expressing gratitude for the people around us, objectification has no room to dominate. I encourage women who are battling lustful thoughts in particular to pray for the person they're tempted to objectify or are already in a moment of objectifying, and then praise God for the gifts of that person, *including* their physical attractiveness. Turning our attention toward praying for the person, even if we don't know them, and praising God for the gift of their life and dignity is the opposite of what objectification is trying to do, which is to turn them into something for us to use and discard without any regard for their humanity.

If affection comes from a deep, abiding delight—an ability to see, even the unlovable, with God's eyes—then rehabilitating affection has to begin with cultivating gratitude. When our first reaction and disposition toward encountering others, whether or not we know them well, is to be grateful for them, the lighthearted and humble affectionate love we crave can have fertile ground to grow. Paradoxically, leaving behind the false comfort of objectifying others brings the true comfort that only virtuous affection can consistently offer.

Recovering Friendship

In Lewis's view, true friendship is incredibly rare. It's the love that allows people to be side by side, united by a common truth, mission, or interest:

> Friendship arises out of mere Companionship when two or more of the companions discover that they have in common some insight or interest or even taste which the others do not share and which, till that moment, each believed to be his own unique treasure (or burden). The typical expression of opening Friendship would be something like, *"What? You too? I thought I was the only one."*[7]

While affection can sit back and delight and demand very little, friendship demands the commonality of caring about something similar—whether an experience, belief, or task. Lewis elaborates further:

> The shared activity and therefore the companionship . . . may be a common religion, common studies, a common profession, even a common recreation. All who share it will be our companions; but one or two or three who share something more will be our Friends.

> In this kind of love, as Emerson said, *"Do you love me?"*
> means . . . *"Do you care about the same truth?"*[8]

The "something more" that Lewis refers to in the above passage is precisely the unique care for a particular uniting factor—whether religion, studies, profession, or recreation, as Lewis summarizes—that goes deeper than a mere common engagement in the thing itself. I have plenty of people who go to my parish or share my Catholic faith, but I count as my closest friends those who devote themselves to practicing it in the same way I've been called to do. It's not just our faith but also our devotion to it that takes us from mere companions to true friends.

The destruction of friendship, in my opinion, mostly comes from the hiding that is so prevalent in sexual sin and addiction. We cannot make true friends while in hiding and in a habit of deception. In order to truly experience love in friendship, we have to be willing to share the missions that matter most to us, including that of recovery. When you're actively trying to recover and heal, there's hardly a mission that matters more; but for women in particular, sometimes *none* of our friends know. In opening up to our friends that we care about the truth of being free and healed in our sexuality, we give them the opportunity to share a similar conviction—or join in ours—thus deepening the love we experience in friendship.

The restoration of friendship is often what I see happening in the small groups I've facilitated, even virtually. Women discover an incredibly powerful love in that of friendship. They recognize their shared mission and the strength of pursuing it shoulder to shoulder with one another. Pursuing the mission of recovery alone isn't just lonely; it's not very effective. But when we open ourselves and our stories to those walking through life and recovery with us, we can see the grounding that love in friendship has to offer us.

Recovering Romance

Romantic or erotic love is defined simply by Lewis as "the state which we call 'being in love'; or, if you prefer, that kind of love which lovers are 'in.'"[9] It's important to distinguish it from mere sexual desire; otherwise, true romantic love can be mistaken for the erotic element that can be a *part* of romantic love but not the whole. Lewis also makes this tangible: "Sexual desire, without Eros, wants *it*—the *thing in itself*; Eros wants the Beloved."[10] Sexual desire left alone wants sexual pleasure, but desire that is subject to true love is good and can be fruitful in fostering that love.

The loss of romantic or erotic love in the midst of sexual sin is precisely in the stopping short at mere sexual desire. Sexual desire isn't the enemy when it's part of a deeper love for a Beloved, but left to its own, it can become all-consuming and lustful, and we can't advance toward a truly communicative and uniting love with the person we desire to be with. Pornography in particular—especially the types that attract and target a large number of women by involving a lot of pseudo-romantic or relational interaction (think of the widespread appeal of *Fifty Shades of Grey* to a female audience)—collapses true romance into base carnality. Even many "romance" movies center the arc of the storyline around when the couple *finally* has sex (looking at you, Nicholas Sparks). Sex becomes the pinnacle of romantic love, not the expression of a desire for total, lifelong unity with the Beloved within the safety of a sacred vow.

The recovery of romance from pornography, masturbation, and sexual sin is often one of the most sensitive topics with the women I've accompanied, as it was sensitive in my own journey. For starters, it's the love that seems most off-limits when you're entrenched in sexual brokenness and sin; the concept of a holy romantic love that includes ordered sexual desire feels completely unattainable. Simultaneously, some women place the healing of their sexuality *solely* in the possibility of a future relationship, thinking that redemption can only come when they have a romantic relationship or get married—or, at least on a basic level, they think their sexual sins will resolve when they're able to have sex with a spouse.

There are a few issues in placing eros on a pedestal, even if it's the dream of a rightly ordered and sanctified eros. First, sex in marriage and sexual sins aren't in the same category—one doesn't replace the other. Sexual sin will not disappear when you're having sex within a marriage. In fact, triggers could be more common, and without any effort at resolution, the compulsions they bring about will sabotage not just the sexual part of the marriage but the marriage as a whole. Sex, even when it's vowed and sacramental, should not be seen as a mere outlet for our lust or compulsions. Instead, addiction, compulsion, and lust should be appropriately addressed before entering marriage; if you're already in a marriage, they should be addressed as swiftly as possible. This doesn't mean perfection—temptation and sin won't disappear. Rather, your mindset switches from sex being a mere outlet to sex being a *gift*.

Second, idealizing a future relationship or expecting your current one to fix your problems is making recovery dependent on the arrival of a person who may never come, or it places unfair pressure on an existing or future relationship. A romantic relationship or marriage cannot redeem you; only Jesus can, and he offers that redemption in the here and now, not on the condition of a future vocation. Further, such idealizing places the idea of romantic love in a position of authority where it doesn't belong. As Lewis clarifies, true romantic love should cause us to recognize its purpose of directing us toward God instead of depending on it as the be-all and end-all. He says,

> The event of falling in love is of such a nature that we
> are right to reject as intolerable the idea that it should
> be transitory. . . . In one high bound it has overleaped
> the massive wall of our selfhood; it has made appe-
> tite itself altruistic, tossed personal happiness aside as
> a triviality and planted the interests of another in the
> center of our being. Spontaneously and without effort
> we have fulfilled the law (towards one person) by loving

> our neighbor as ourselves. It is an image, a foretaste, of
> what we must become to all if Love Himself rules in us
> without a rival.[11]

Lewis essentially suggests that the person who is completely surrendered to God isn't "in love" with everyone in a romantic, sexual sense, but the prioritization and desire for unity with the other that characterizes romantic love become directed toward not just one person but everyone. In heaven, when the faithful are united eternally in the love of God, our love won't be partial; we'll be in perfect unity with God and one another, rid of earthly limitations. Romantic love on earth, when rightly ordered and experienced in grace, is an incredibly tangible foretaste of this. It's not meant to be the end in itself.

This is why a future romantic relationship or marriage can't become the hope of recovery or the condition that recovery is placed under. Rather, working to recover romantic love with Christ himself first is key—not to mention, available to every woman regardless of her state in life. Placing our need for romantic love and our sexual desire under Jesus's blessing and allowing him to use it to guide us toward a deeper relationship with him is what will truly recover romance. No one human being will be able to be the space where we make sense of our brokenness. As I shared in my own story earlier, it wasn't a romantic relationship that I needed in order to recover and heal; it was friendship, charity, affection, *and* romantic love, but romantic love with Christ first.

Recovering Charity

Charity is the pinnacle of a supernatural love—the love of God ultimately characterized by complete self-donation. As we advance in the Christian life, we are called to this kind of love for both God and others. Charity is willing to sacrifice all for the sake of love, particularly Love himself. As already discussed above, this means diving into the vulnerability, risks, and pain inherent to sacrificial love. Lewis describes what happens to the human heart closed off to charity out of fear of pain:

> There is no safe investment. To love at all is to be vulnerable. Love anything, and your heart will certainly be wrung and possibly broken. If you want to make sure of keeping it intact, you must give your heart to no one, not even to an animal. Wrap it carefully round with hobbies and little luxuries; avoid all entanglements; lock it up safe in the casket or coffin of your selfishness. But in that casket—safe, dark, motionless, airless—it will change. It will not be broken; it will become unbreakable, impenetrable, irredeemable. The alternative to tragedy, or at least to the risk of tragedy, is damnation. The only place outside of heaven where you can be perfectly safe from all the dangers and perturbations of love is hell.[12]

I've seen this passage quoted often, but usually without the last line: "The only place outside of heaven where you can be perfectly safe from the dangers and perturbations of love is hell." To me, this might be the most important sentence of the entire passage. Lewis is driving home the truth that if we're looking for a life without the pain of love, we're looking for hell. But if we're willing to be broken open for love, we have the hope of heaven, where the pain, suffering, and breaking will cease.

Of all the loves, this is the most difficult to put into words. Sexual sin is a massive roadblock to charity, just as other sins are, but it takes the denial of self-donation to a physical and sexual level, not just an interior one. *Gaudium et Spes*, one of the foundational documents of the Second Vatican Council, says that "man, who is the only creature on earth which God willed for itself, cannot fully find himself except through a sincere gift of himself" (24:3). Without the risk and vulnerability of love, man is literally not capable of becoming *who he is*. The sanctification and completion of his very self is dependent on the invitation to give himself for love, which is inherent to his nature. Every person, regardless of their state in life or history of sin, is invited to love and be loved, thus finding themselves, in the way that only God can supply.

Our Lord will invite each of us individually and uniquely to this self-donation in charity, and he'll do it in several different ways, if we allow him. Whether it's through our work; entering a vocation to marriage, consecration, or religious life; or the everyday suffering we face, he asks us to die to ourselves for the sake of love. The ways we're asked to die will be radical and ordinary, big and small, excruciating and annoying, but they will all sanctify and lead us toward eternal happiness if we say yes to the invitation.

Once the human heart has tasted the agape love of God, it's hard for sexual sin to ever be as satisfying again. This doesn't mean we never engage in these sins again, not to mention are tempted by them, but they lose their luster once we see the capability of our hearts to be broken in the most beautiful and satisfying way by the real, raw love that we truly crave. One woman in recovery articulated it simply to me: "It's not that I'm not tempted to go back there—I am. I just don't *want* to go back there. It's a dark place." Once our hearts have encountered light—even if it's just a sliver—we're able to know darkness isn't our home. We know in the deepest part of ourselves that it's only in self-gift that we can find who we are, and that will *always* call to us.

In one of our first conversations, I was sharing my pessimistic feelings about the world and its decay with my now-husband. (Just your average conversation with a potential love interest, I guess?) He responded: "Rachael, the human heart never changes . . . so there's always hope." He's repeated it many times since, and he's right: we will always be beckoned by the call to love, no matter how far from it we are. Recovering charity is the hardest because none of us truly has it down—not until heaven. But once your heart is broken open by love, even for the briefest moment, you'll know that there's no turning back. Sexual sin won't have the same grip on you, even if the patterns continue.

A breakup and a band of rowdy teenagers broke my heart open and gave me a taste of the call that I will be striving to fulfill for the rest of my life—to say no to all things that tell me my desire comes first and say yes to the invitation of God to be broken and poured out for love, whether in affection, friendship, romance, or ultimately charity. I have been broken open many times since, and I have no doubt I'll need it many more times on my road to eternity. But after encountering the beautiful, aching pain of real love, I know that there's no other way.

If you're still entrenched in sexual sin and looking for that taste of love, go out and *seek* it. Give yourself away—in friendship, relationship, meaningful work, volunteering, ministry, and involvement in causes that matter to you. "Give until it hurts," as St. Teresa of Calcutta said. God's love is waiting, but we cannot lock ourselves up and expect it to come to our airless casket. Take one step out in love, however meager it may seem, and watch the love of God come for you—to break your heart, yes, but ultimately to help you become who you are.

7
WEARING YOUR FACE

The hands of the king are the hands of a healer, and so shall the rightful king be known.

–J. R. R. Tolkien

Stepping into Leadership

My later college years brought more and more opportunities to share my story, with increasing responses, particularly from other women on my campus. After one talk I gave toward the end of my junior year, so many women approached me afterward to share their own stories of sexual addiction and sin, or to ask for help, that the idea of a support group became tough to ignore.

I pitched the concept to campus ministry without much idea of how I'd pull it off. It took a few months to get the group fine-tuned to women's needs, instead of being a joint group with the men. Once we had divided the groups and the men's leader and I had made a plan for a launch, I scoured the internet for any sort of program or book we could use as a guide, and I found nothing. I wrote most of our small-group curriculum while sitting in class. (Don't tell my professors—though they probably could tell.)

I plowed forward with a zeal and conviction that I was helping set women free, even if others didn't recognize the struggle to begin with. A lot of people gave me funny or surprised reactions when I talked about the group, including some in school leadership. At one point, my co-leader, Mary Jo, and I made our own promotional posters because we couldn't get them approved as long as they had the word *pornography* printed on them.

It all felt more than a bit rebellious. Mary Jo and I felt a thrill as we taped our posters to every dorm door, inviting each woman on campus to come to the launch event for the support groups. When the night came for the launch, three times as many women showed up than men. They were hungry for recovery themselves or longing to learn how to be women who could accompany others in this issue. It was nothing short of inspiring.

That first support group was one of the sweetest communities I've ever had the privilege of being a part of. It was made up of women ranging from freshmen to seniors, and we couldn't have been more different. There were distinct and unique personalities, interests, and social circles, but the unity that chasing recovery and healing provided was deep, and we all felt it. I knew that we had tapped into something, and it was a model that I would turn to a few years down the road when I started my larger ministry.

I say all of this to point out that while I was stepping into a rewarding, fulfilling place of ministry and mentorship, and discussing my struggles was becoming more and more of an everyday part of life, I still carried the awkwardness and discomfort in my sexuality that had been with me since my childhood. Talking about my story became more of a tool to mentor with rather than something I could truly be vulnerable about. I still experienced vulnerability with close friends in talking about my struggles, and I was able to open up somewhat in our support group, but I took—regrettably—a somewhat performative stance. I was far more comfortable being seen as a rebel or trailblazer than someone who was still incredibly wounded and who let her actions be dictated by those wounds—and in need of deep healing.

Though my discomfort with my femininity was beginning to fade, it would still flare up as I tried to enter into dating again.

After a couple of years of being single, and even wrestling deeply with what I thought was a call to religious life, going out on dates again was strange. But the resurrection of my discomfort made it stranger. It felt contradictory: I had ownership of my story at that point; it was even public knowledge on campus that I was the leader of the support group and was open to talking to any female student in need of help. Yet in the face of relationships with men, I didn't feel I had ownership; I still felt fearful, awkward, and like a fish out of water.

Into the Deep

After graduation and leading that recovery ministry for a year, I experienced a spike in anxiety that sent me to a Catholic therapist for the summer while I lived at home with my parents and began my master's degree. Once again, it felt contradictory. I thought I had dealt with anxiety, for the most part, over a year prior to this spike, which I know now was partially a major withdrawal symptom from no longer consuming pornography to numb myself. I felt as if I had a plan for the next year of my life by going to grad school and enjoying the exciting opportunities waiting for me afterward. Instead of joyful anticipation, I experienced a resurgence of crippling fear and anxiety, to the point of losing sleep.

Resolved to go back to therapy for more work on anxiety, I got connected with a young, incredibly gentle, and intuitive therapist who noticed something in my intake form.

"I see you've had unwanted sexual experiences," she said. "Do you want to talk about that?"

I explained that I had hesitated to even check that box because I had worked through those experiences already with the counselor on my college campus, who had called them what they were: abuse. I had wept back in my dorm after hearing that word applied to my memories. But the counselor also asked some repeated questions and used methods I was uncomfortable with, so I stopped seeing her. Maybe I thought hearing the word was enough; I just needed to forgive and move on. But my new therapist pressed deeper.

"Are you sure that's resolved?" she asked gently. "I'd like to hear more details, if you're willing to share them."

I recounted the memories for her as best I could, and she confirmed that they were indeed abusive experiences. "Often we don't use the term *abuse* because we don't believe our experiences are severe enough. But that's false," she reassured me. "People who had more power or strength than you used that power and strength to take advantage of you, whether they realized it or not. That's the definition of abuse."

I nodded, once again feeling choked up but relieved at her gentleness.

"Rachael, I'd like to continue looking at this, if you're willing," she said. "I think there might be a link here to what you're feeling now."

There certainly was a link. With that therapist's gentle guidance, I was able to unpack the lies that I had been holding within me from each of those experiences—that I wasn't safe, that my body was made to feel discomfort or cause others discomfort, and that my sexuality was inherently damaged. After each session I was able to spend time in adoration at the counseling center or a nearby parish and work through the session in the presence of Jesus. Sometimes it involved working through memories while imagining him there and what he would say or do in response to my pain and shame. The lies I had believed didn't feel silenced until I had allowed Jesus into those memories with me, though it was a painful process to go there.

Early on, I shared with my therapist about my addiction to pornography, and she was also able to connect the dots between it and my earlier experiences in a concrete way that I had never realized before. Though I knew there was some connection, I wasn't able to see the direct correlation between the lies that I had carried with me as a child and the ways pornography seemed to calm, answer, or even reinforce them. I find this to be the case often, with many women other than myself. Though we know there's a connection somewhere, it often takes another pair of eyes on our story to truly see the relationship between our childhood experiences—sexual or otherwise—and our current addictions and compulsions.

As she put it, I was "primed for pornography to make an entrance into my life." Hearing that didn't take away the fact that I was responsible for the sins I had committed, but it helped me see the specific ways that pornography met me in my deep-seated feelings and wounds in my sexuality. I have found over and over again that each woman whose story I've encountered has a similar connection—in some way, we were all "primed." Whether it's by abuse, neglect, or education that either overexposed us to sexuality or didn't give us necessary information—thus leaving us to our own devices—we all have a reason why pornography, masturbation, or other compulsions showed up and addressed a need. Even if that need was simply pleasure or soothing stress or boredom, there's a bottomless well of aching need in the human person, and all of our pursuits—sinful or otherwise—are attempts to fill that well.

One of the most common questions I get after giving a talk or in emails is just simply how to "get free" or "get rid of" pornography or masturbation. I remember using similar language myself. But as my own journey of healing has gone deeper and deeper, I've realized how much that question stops short of the real issue. Sometimes in addressing our addictions, we become addicted to finding the one answer or one solution that can save us. Our desperation can be a sign that we're convicted of the havoc and damage pornography and masturbation are wreaking on our lives, but it can also be a sign that we haven't yet surrendered, because one of the most fundamental steps of surrender is allowing the Lord to actually address and heal the wounds and needs that began our addiction in the first place.

This is why it's incredibly difficult to try to give anyone a "blueprint" of recovery—because I can't. My own story of recovery is deeply imperfect, riddled with error and beauty. Each person who walks the road of healing themselves could probably say the same thing.

Letting the Mask Fall

Though my college years took me on an incredible journey of discovering a life of intimacy with Christ and I was experiencing sobriety from my pornography addiction, I was still hiding from the pain of my woundedness in sexuality and the fear and anxiousness it created. Ministry, ironically, sometimes creates the safest place to hide from the deep work that's needed to actually heal. It took my anxiety and fear overpowering me, and the gentle guidance of a very devout therapist, for me to finally allow the Lord to begin to take me to the source.

In different classes I've taken on sexual addiction and counseling, one of the overarching messages was "Freedom from addiction is not about sobriety; it's about intimacy." Sobriety is an honorable and noble goal, but it isn't sustainable without recovering the intimacy that our souls were created for. Without that intimacy, our woundedness will find another outlet to express itself.

A few months ago, I spent some time on a small Catholic college campus meeting one-on-one with students for a day leading up to a talk. One young woman walked into the room, immediately striking me with her bright blue eyes and gentle smile. Usually in these one-on-ones, women are nervous or ashamed, sometimes struggling to hold eye contact. This girl looked me straight in the eye the entire time we talked, composed and quietly confident. When I asked, "What's up? How can I help you today?" she replied simply, "I'm not sure. I think I just want to share my story, if that's okay."

Her self-awareness of why her struggles with sexual sin happened was stunning to me. She laid out her story chronologically, tracing one of her main wounds back to her relationship with her father and the ways her femininity had seemed like a burden to him. "I decided it would be better if I was a boy," she told me. "So I became as much like a boy as possible." Even more stunning than her awareness of her wounds and their effects was her awareness of Christ's healing of her heart and the ways she had welcomed him into her story. She smiled as she recounted the ways his love had shown itself to her and the ways she was learning to grow and become comfortable with her expression of femininity. More than anything, she just wanted someone to marvel with.

Seeing this level of honesty and awe was convicting for me. It reminded me of that summer with my therapist when, for what felt like the first time, I saw my story through the lens of God's love instead of shame. Like the wise young college freshman who is clearly ahead of the game, I was given the chance to marvel at the work and kindness of God as he wiped the dust off of my feminine heart. There was an achingly beautiful pain to that summer. It was as if I could feel reality and integration pouring from the inside out.

C. S. Lewis (if you're wondering when I'm going to stop referencing Lewis, the answer is not anytime soon) has a poignant work of fiction titled *Till We Have Faces*. It's a retelling of the myth of Cupid and Psyche, centered on a princess who is born incredibly ugly. This princess faces many sufferings throughout her life—loss, unrequited love, and neglect—and her heart becomes deeply embittered toward the gods as a result. The book is written from her point of view as a complaint against the gods, but when she finally has a vision in which the opportunity arises to read her complaint, it comes out as nothing. Lewis explains the reason why:

> When the time comes to you at which you will be forced at last to utter the speech which has lain at the center of your soul for years, which you have, all that time, idiot-like, been saying over and over, you'll not talk about the joy of words. I saw well why the gods do not speak to us openly, nor let us answer. Till that word can be dug out of us, why should they hear the babble that we think we mean? How can they meet us face to face till we have faces?[1]

The princess, in her suffering, thought her grievances toward the gods were her loss and suffering, but really, deep down, it was the wound of ugliness and rejection she had carried with her throughout her entire life. This wound informed the way she *approached* her suffering and received it. And through the lens of rejection, her suffering could be received only as more rejection from the Divine.

In college, I asked a professor of mine who is a scholar of Lewis to interpret this passage for me after reading it for the first time, and his response was jarring but poignant: "It's only after you realize how dark you are, and how much you actually hate yourself, that you can begin to be loved." Lewis's words speak to my own experience of unearthing the wounds that had driven me toward pornography as well as those of the wise college freshman who traced her sexual sin back to rejection of her femininity. Oftentimes, the weaknesses and brokenness we think we have aren't what's going on at all. In every human experience there are many "one words" that we say over and over through our sin. We proclaim our rejection, abandonment, abuse, loneliness, or fear without recognizing that healing can only come from digging up those wounds themselves, not just tackling the sins that express them.

Shame also keeps us trapped in this cycle. Even if we're in a period of sobriety from our behaviors, we have shame over having battled them in the first place, not to mention the shame from those original wounds themselves. Shame tells us not to go deeper into our own hearts because we won't like what we find there, or worse—we will not be able to withstand it. It'll overpower and overwhelm us. Particularly when you've believed the lie that your soul itself *creates* the feeling of "dirtiness" that so regularly accompanies sexual sin, it feels especially threatening to explore the wounds and workings of that soul. We become so used to calling shame home that we hesitate to even try to leave it behind. As Hans Urs von Balthasar said, also using the imagery of a mask while addressing Christ: "And if you were to try to burst my prison door open from the outside, from the inside I would resist you with clairvoyant despair. The mask and my face have inter-grown."[2]

So many women I've journeyed with long for a face-to-face encounter with God that can heal them, but that cannot happen unless we are willing to actually *wear* our face before him. If we approach God solely with the goal of arresting and "getting rid of" our sexual compulsions and unwanted behaviors, maybe we'll succeed in breaking an addiction or habit, but we won't heal. The wounds that drove us there in the first place, plus the wounds we inflicted on ourselves through sinning, will continue to fester and express themselves elsewhere, especially if fear and shame make us continue to refuse the hand of God reaching into those wounds. We cannot speak to God face-to-face until we are willing to reveal our own face to him, no matter how ugly, marred, or shameful it may seem to us. He wants to address our sin, yes, but more than that, he wants to gaze with love on what we're holding in our heart of hearts. We have to be willing to confront those very experiences that have left us feeling confused, rejected, ashamed, abandoned, powerless, and dirty. We have to even be willing to experience the hatred and disgust that recalling those experiences brings along with them—but experience those things while being held safely in the arms of the Father.

Truth be told, I was still living in a rejection of my femininity, or my sexuality as a part of my being. It was a place of darkness and fear for me, perhaps even one of hatred. My anxiety stemmed from several places, one being this rejection and fear. Anxiety, in all its forms, convinces you that you are not safe—and to me, being feminine was not safe. In fact, it was the place I had experienced the most blatant, obvious sin in my life thus far. How could I love something that seemed so entrenched? It felt best, even subconsciously, to just let it lie. But letting it lie meant denying a part of my being, and that would never lead to lasting peace.

We live in a "self-love" culture, where the highest form of love we're encouraged to seek is that which we can give ourselves. Yet, we're a culture that's more depraved, superficial, and depressed than ever. When we are not the source of Love, we can hardly be depended upon to offer enough love to completely heal and satisfy anyone, *especially* ourselves. Sexual addiction and woundedness are two places where this tension perhaps becomes most clear: your love is human and damaged, and subject to temptation that can lead you to sin. Broken love cannot heal broken love—only the source of Love can. As my professor made clear, that love cannot be experienced until we acknowledge the darkness and hatred we feel.

Digging up the deep fear of and discomfort with my femininity was at times excruciatingly painful, but those therapy sessions and holy hours afterward finally gave me the space to let my mask fall and to wear my face. There can certainly be a darkness one experiences in this process of letting the mask fall and true healing work its way deep into the soul. Consolation can feel rare during the process, and the emotions we experience can be overwhelming. It's easy to collapse our faith into what we might be feeling or thinking in those moments of being crushed or overwhelmed by the weight of finally letting things out, rather than relying on belief beyond our understanding. It was gut-wrenching and mentally exhausting to admit it: I was a recovering addict who was incredibly uncomfortable with my sexuality, and I felt I had never known anything different, nor ever would know anything different. Experiencing the fullness of love—in affection, friendship, and especially eros—felt impossible for me. No ministry, job, opportunity, or performance could diminish that—only he could. That summer required me to admit to God that there were some parts of myself that I saw as ugly, irredeemable, and without hope, even if I was sober from the sinful behaviors that had caused me so much shame. Only in finally saying these things aloud—whether in counseling or in prayer—did the tender voice of Jesus have the chance to reply, and reply he did. For the first time in my life, I was able to hear and receive his love for my womanhood and express femininity without discomfort and fear.

The freedom that came as a result of these encounters with Jesus also had an incredible effect on my interactions with others, including men. By the grace of God, I met my husband during that summer of healing, and the difference I felt in his presence was tangible. I wasn't consumed by the old framework I had for my sexuality. I didn't feel awkward or out of place. I didn't want to run. Instead, I was able to enjoy being pursued by and dating him in a way I never thought was possible for me. It was not perfect, not even close—but it was *good*, and I felt it.

Intimacy, Not Just Sobriety

When I was asked to write this book, I knew that it partly needed to be practical, but I also don't think a self-help book is all women need when addressing sexual addiction. For a long time, our approach in the Church chiefly focused on these practical areas: how to stop watching porn, stop masturbating, stop lustful behavior, just *stop*. There's value to that, but again, that's sobriety, not intimacy. There's a time and place for the practical, especially when you're simply trying to enter recovery. But simply "stopping" whatever compulsion is taking over your life is not the end. In order to truly heal and integrate our sexuality, as the Church calls us to, we have to be willing to dive deep into the wounds and beliefs that have been leading us to compulsion, sometimes for years.

When we put our relationship with God in the context of a human relationship, some of our habits with him are revealed for what they actually are: avoidance of intimacy. If my marriage only contained conversations where my husband and I discussed ways we can improve things around our home, at work, or in our personal lives—essentially, how our "habits" can change— our marriage would be stagnant and lifeless. Instead, just like a marriage, intimacy with God can only deepen if we allow ourselves to be seen as we truly are. The vulnerability that wearing your face takes doesn't just mean times of painful revealing and encountering the self-hatred, disgust, anger, or other repulsive things in ourselves. It means the moments of joyful encounter with God too. But one cannot happen without the other. You cannot deny your femininity, whether in abusing it for sinful purposes or hiding it out of fear, because to deny your sexuality is to deny the reality that you are *human*. We cannot escape the condition in which we were created. We can only dive in to both the glory and the devastation that we exist in as human beings. As Lewis says in *Prince Caspian* through the character of Aslan: "You come of the Lord Adam and the Lady Eve . . . and that is both honour enough to erect the head of the poorest beggar, and shame enough to bow the shoulders of the greatest emperor on earth. Be content."[3]

8
THE GATEWAY DRUGS

In your struggle against sin you have not yet
resisted to the point of shedding blood.

–Hebrews 12:4

Once, when speaking with a friend in an older generation than mine, she commented how incredibly difficult it must be to struggle with pornography in the modern world. "In my day it was just magazines," she said. "Now it's . . . everywhere." She's not wrong: sexual addiction is difficult to recover from on its own, but it's only become more so as our culture becomes increasingly sexualized. Everywhere we turn, triggers are available to us in the form of media, music, and advertisements, just to name a few.

Perhaps the prominence of sexually triggering content is obvious, but what isn't always obvious are what I call the "gateway drugs" to pornography and other sexual compulsions—seemingly unrelated things that are easier to make excuses for. This list contains things that were triggering for my own recovery journey or have regularly been triggering for women I've walked with.

1. Social Media

The fact that exposure to porn can regularly happen through social media aside, the very presence of social media in your life during recovery can be incredibly triggering. It's also perhaps the most difficult trigger to truly get rid of.

Even if you're not accessing pornographic content through social media (which certain platforms make it remarkably easy to do), the very nature of social media is enough to keep you in a cycle of addiction. Jaron Lanier, an influential Silicon Valley tech who wrote the brilliant book *Ten Arguments for Deleting Your Social Media Accounts Right Now*, unequivocally says that "we're being hypnotized little by little by technicians we can't see, for purposes we don't know. We're all lab animals now."[1] The discussion surrounding social media has become more and more prominent, with documentaries like *The Social Dilemma*— which featured Lanier and other Silicon Valley techs or former social media executives and engineers—also bringing to light the addictive motivations of social media companies. Whether you like it or not, social media companies are just that: companies. They have money to make, and *you* and your time are the ways that these companies make that money. As *The Social Dilemma* aptly states, "If you are not paying for the product, then you are the product."[2]

It's in the best interest of companies like Meta (Facebook, Instagram, WhatsApp), Pinterest, Twitter, Snapchat, and TikTok to absorb as much of your time as possible. When they do, they make more money—it's as simple as that. Because of this, I think there are many discussions to be had in the Church about whether we should so readily embrace social media and consider it morally neutral, when there's an increasing amount of evidence that these private companies use their platforms for malicious purposes— even just, at a base level, the manipulation of human thought and behavior. Whatever those discussions might conclude for the Church as a whole, it's clear that social media's goal of stealing as much time as possible, while tying a person to a device, is the last thing in the world that a recovering porn addict needs.

During my junior year of college, I ended up deleting Snapchat (the only social media platform I still had) because it began to feature articles from outlets like *Cosmopolitan* that were sexual in nature, typically giving some form of sex advice. While I wasn't reading or watching pornography anymore, I would find myself still scrolling through articles on sex that I had no business reading. Instead of addressing my itch to consume sexual content, I gave it a small outlet in those articles. To make matters worse, they updated them daily. They were easier to write off than porn because they were "advice," right? But as an unmarried practicing Catholic committed to abstinence unless I did get married, it was advice I *definitely* didn't need.

Once again, whether the content you're consuming is still somewhat sexual in nature—like what I found on Snapchat—if you're on social media, you are consuming content nonetheless, and that content is probably addicting. Whether it's home-design feeds, memes, fashion ideas, or even Catholic influencers, we each have our kryptonite on our social media platforms. When you're a recovering porn addict, you don't just need to keep an eye out for sexual content; you need to keep an eye out for that kryptonite that keeps a device in your hand, no matter what it is. I found myself even needing to delete the news app on my phone at one point in college—first, because it was depressing and, second, because it kept me at the beck and call of my curiosity while supplying my phone as the answer to that curiosity.

I am incredibly skeptical of anyone who talks about their "good relationship" with social media. Their phrasing sounds oddly like an addict's: "I can give it up whenever I want." I don't doubt that some people manage their time better or don't find social media as attractive, but what I'm sure of is that I don't know a human being walking the earth who is above temptation, sexual or otherwise. To believe that you alone are strong enough, holy enough, or smart enough to stand up to experts in tech development, engineering, and psychology teaming up to create a platform strikes me as naive. Even to say that you use social media to access formative content for your faith doesn't change the fact that you are still using it and therefore subject to the motivations of private companies, even if you avoid their manipulations more often than not. To put it simply, no one is entirely in the driver's seat of their social media accounts and usage—no one. The very fact that most of us constantly have to put time limits or other things in place to keep us in check proves it. No matter what we're looking at, social media is doing its job.

The goal in recovery from addiction is not to replace one addiction with another. If you are in recovery from an attachment or addiction to pornography, masturbation, or another sexual compulsion, be on the lookout for social media—or just media in general—to try to offer itself as a substitute. One woman I know shared that whenever she goes on TikTok or Instagram, she can't resist binging, and even though she isn't looking at anything pornographic, the very act of being on her phone for that long creates a similar amount of exhaustion and shame as watching porn did for her. This isn't because, again, she watched something inherently sinful but because her conscience is pricked by the cycle of addiction that she's known before. I can relate. Even today, I can be tempted to distract myself from emotions like stress, pain, sadness, or boredom—some of those the same emotions that would frequently send me to porn as a teenager—with binge-watching a show or reading useless content on the internet. And if I do it, I feel a similar tone of shame and defeat that I used to feel after watching porn. I don't even have social media anymore (save LinkedIn), but they're not the only platforms committed to demanding my time. Netflix and others are perpetrators too. Reed Hastings, the CEO of Netflix, famously said that their "greatest competitor is sleep."[3] Disappearing into a digital abyss is too easy to do, instead of facing life head-on and allowing myself to live in reality, even when that reality is simply just needing to go to sleep. It is in our fallen nature to hide from God and reality, and distraction is simply another form of hiding.

There's also something major to be said about rediscovering and protecting your solitude as you heal and recover. Sexual sin and promiscuity are so deeply founded upon use of the human person that the concept of personal solitude can be severely damaged when we're struggling with an addiction. Solitude isn't isolation; it's the state of being in communion with God. In *Brave New World*, Aldous Huxley depicted an eerie society with several mantras, one being "Everybody belongs to everyone else."[4] Ultimately Huxley showed a society that had completely dispensed with solitude and gave no one the ability to find it. This particular mantra of "belonging" was behind the commonplace sexual promiscuity accepted in the fictional culture (sound familiar?), but it's food for thought when it comes to social media. Your very *life* is sacred, not just your sexuality and body, and solitude is the very place we receive or are rerooted in a recognition of our God-given dignity. Pornography and sexual sin cheapen sexuality and the body, thereby cheapening the dignity of human life, but so do practices that keep nothing about our lives sacred or private. When every moment is at the mercy of being posted and commented on by others, and our lives become fodder for social media feeds instead of real experiences that are just *lived*, we're "belonging to everybody else" in a way we shouldn't. Even if we *aren't* posting everything or even often, the very existence of our accounts means that there's always the potential. And when you're trying to rediscover your dignity and the dignity of others by recovering solitude, just that potential can be harmful in itself.

I think Lanier said it best: "To free yourself, to be more authentic, to be less addicted, to be less manipulated, to be less paranoid . . . for all these marvelous reasons, delete your accounts."[5]

2. Romantic Movies (or Books)

I want to begin on this behemoth by first saying that some movies and books *do* contain pornography, as we covered in an earlier chapter. If a sex scene is shown in a movie, whether the sexual activity is explicitly shown or implied through sounds, facial expressions, and movements, it has the potential to be incredibly arousing for the viewer, particularly a female viewer who is more likely to be aroused by auditory content or content that leaves something to the imagination. Likewise, descriptions of sexual activity in books can also be pornographic in nature and similarly utilize the female tendency for arousal through imagination.

However, even if a movie or book does not involve a clear sex scene, a majority of movies and TV shows involve some harmful sexual undertones. In most rom-coms or romantic dramas, the couple having sex is a major plot point, and there's a significant emotional buildup to them doing so. Even if the sex scene isn't shown, the fact that a plot, or a decent part of it, revolves around it should be concerning for women in recovery. Remember that we're trying to reorder our love, not just achieve sobriety. Feeding ourselves content that makes romance and sex interchangeable, or makes emotional connection revolve around sexual chemistry, keeps us in a place of seeking pleasure over sacrifice and lust over love.

Another harmful attitude that comes up often in movies and TV shows is that of making sex incredibly casual, including just constant sexual humor. Hookups are normalized and encouraged, and sex has little to no meaning in a relationship. Even if nothing is, again, depicted on-screen, the constant sexual banter or details of the sex lives of main characters does the trick when it comes to keeping your mind in the gutter. Especially if you're trying to recover from pornography, learning to protect your thoughts from oversexualized imagery and language becomes the name of the game. The more casualized sex is in a movie or TV show, the more food for thought it provides—or the more it makes your already hard-to-battle sexual thoughts seem normal and commonplace.

It's okay to be strict about your media—always—but it's especially okay when in recovery from sexual addiction and compulsion. What you consume in movies, TV shows, and even music matters to your soul, *deeply*. You are not completely unaffected by the media you take in—quite the opposite, in fact. What we allow to fill our minds plays a major role in dictating how we perceive the world and what we think about, and it affects our discernment between vice and virtue. It's incredibly easy to consume media that isn't virtuous; it's much more difficult to comb through the muck and find things that are positive or at the very least aren't harmful—and what's harmful can be very individual. When you're a recovering addict, even watching or reading romantic movies or books that show too much making out or depict foreplay, even between a married couple, can be detrimental to your recovery if it's triggering to you. If you are going to watch a movie or show, don't be afraid to be that nerd who reads a review beforehand to know whether there's going to be content that's difficult for you to say no to (I still read movie reviews meticulously, mostly because I like to spoil the ending . . .) or watch it with a friend you trust to filter.

However you choose to handle your media intake, only you can know what's triggering for you, and you're responsible for walking into something you *know* will be triggering beforehand. If it's too much, delete your streaming service accounts. I promise, life can go on without Netflix. Try to fill time that you filled with media with something new and life-giving. Maybe it's a new exercise routine, that musical instrument you've always wanted to learn to play, or picking up a good book (more on how this helps restore your imagination later). It's important to replace one habit with another, as we've spoken about before. Find positive things to feed your mind in the place of rom-coms, "binge-worthy" shows, or that novel you know you should put down.

3. Toxic Relationships

I've seen it be almost impossible for a woman to recover from sexual addiction and compulsion if her partner is entrenched and unwilling to do anything about it. You can be profoundly dedicated to your own recovery process, but as long as you maintain a close romantic relationship with someone who is refusing to do so for themselves, you will continue to be dragged down in the short or long term. This section pertains to relationships where the couple isn't married; when vows are involved, things become obviously more complex. But if you're dating or engaged and your boyfriend or fiancé is apathetic toward sexual sin—whether individually or as a couple—it's best for your recovery to offer an ultimatum for the relationship: either you need to call it off or he needs to get in the game.

There is a *massive* difference between struggling on the road to chastity and not caring about it at all. I know wonderful couples adamantly pursuing holiness who fell many times in the sexual aspect of their relationship before being married. The determinant of virtue in a relationship when it comes to chastity isn't whether you are perfect; it's whether you seek forgiveness from God and each other when you make a mistake and take responsibility for that mistake by doing your best to prevent it from happening again. A relationship that brings you closer to virtue—even if it's difficult and rocky—is a relationship worth staying in, if there's peace. The toxic ones are where you feel you're on the road alone or trying to drag a partner along.

You should not have to convince someone that chastity matters or that your recovery matters. It's not acceptable for a partner to continue allowing pornography and sin to influence your relationship without resisting it or to take a "you do you" approach to recovery. If he's addicted too and is content remaining so, it's healthiest for you to leave the relationship behind, not just for your long-term recovery but also for your soul. Conversely, giving him the chance to step up first by supporting you in your efforts to recover, as well as putting in effort himself, is important and could be a motivation to pursue a more virtuous relationship as a whole. Just as I've seen many couples prioritizing sanctity struggle with chastity, I've seen relationships that are apathetic toward sexual sin experience an awakening and make inspiring changes. Everyone deserves a chance to make those changes, but if you invite your partner to do so and it's either pushed off or outright refused, it's time to reconsider the relationship.

On a purely mental or emotional level, it's also worth evaluating whether your relationship is toxic in other ways that cause you stress, shame, or undue pain. Love is rightfully painful insofar as it's purifying in calling us to sacrifice, but it shouldn't cause agonizing emotional pain that's detrimental to your mental, emotional, or spiritual health. If you're trying to recover and your relationship is a source of strife or anxiety, it's also worth discerning if this is the right relationship to be in at the moment—particularly if these emotions are triggering for you. Even if your relationship is spotless when it comes to sexual sin, it can be harmful and sinful in so many other ways. Pay attention to the fruit of your relationship in realms other than chastity. Does this relationship bring you peace? Do you feel you're growing, both in your strengths and how you perceive and handle your weaknesses? Do you feel confident in this person's presence? Can you argue respectfully? All of these things may not seem linked to recovery, but anxiety, insecurity, apathy, or disrespect can all keep someone in a cycle of seeking comfort in the wrong places.

Whenever a woman asks me what should be done in a situation where their boyfriend or fiancé is apathetic toward sexual sin and addiction—as in, they either don't see the immorality of their behavior or make excuses for it while presenting a facade of recovery—I present the above and beg them to prioritize their relationship with Christ and their own recovery. It breaks my heart, but in situations where I hear more details and advise them to consider ending the relationship, the conversation usually ends there. As women, we beautifully value our relationships and fight for them. But we shouldn't do so when our own souls and health are on the line. If your relationship is dragging you down, you typically don't need to be told. You just need to act.

One of my favorite songs is "Sigh No More" by Mumford and Sons. There's a line repeated many times in the chorus that says, "Love—it will not betray you, dismay you, or enslave you; it will set you free—be more like the man you were made to be." The line pierces me every time. Love does not trap you, whether it's in habitual sin, a state of apathy, or being disrespected. It sets you free, because you're deserving of freedom. If you don't have that freedom in a relationship, leave and go find it.

4. Scrupulosity

I don't think I knew the definition of scrupulosity until about high school, and by then I was already experiencing it. St. Ignatius of Loyola defined scrupulosity simply as "when I freely decide that that is sin which is not sin."[6] A scrupulous conscience is one that is constantly guilt-ridden or questioning whether an action is sinful, particularly to the point of anxiety or compulsively practicing devotions in the hope of assuaging guilt.

I've noticed a high percentage of women in recovery from sexual sin struggle with scrupulosity, myself included. At first it may enter as a guard against falling back into patterns of sexual compulsion. It may seem safer to be scrupulous instead of going back to the dark place of being stuck. However, scrupulosity can be a major proponent of shame and send us right back to where we came from, not to mention be incredibly harmful to our spiritual life. Constantly thinking about or fearing sin can, in a way, become a self-fulfilling prophecy. Many women who are scrupulous have articulated a similar pattern: they're extremely meticulous about falling into a sexual sin, whether that's a lustful thought, watching porn, or masturbating, to the point of a scrupulous anxiety or guilt that controls every aspect of their day. However, once they *do* fall, the attitude quickly switches to "Well, I've already fallen, so why not fall again?" and they continue to engage in their behaviors until they go to Confession and start the cycle all over again. The enemy loves to keep us in extremes—either a deep anxiety about our sin or an apathy toward it. One contributes to the other, and sometimes we can flip-flop between them incredibly quickly.

When you're trying to recover, be on your guard against the shiny exterior that scrupulosity can advertise, because beneath it's quite the beast. If you find yourself constantly fearing sexual sin or compulsion, try speaking to a priest or therapist about those worries. Scrupulosity, especially in extreme circumstances, can also be an indication of another mental disorder, such as obsessive-compulsive disorder (OCD). It's important to seek the proper professional assistance if you're experiencing debilitating scrupulosity, what some psychologists even call "religious OCD."

Whether your scrupulosity is extreme or not, it can take time to make peace with the fact that sexual temptation and sin will still be a part of your life, even if you have years of distance between you and addiction. It's important for your journey toward sanctity to take responsibility and repent when you *actually* sin, but it can be a hindrance to your growth to take responsibility for things that aren't sins. Knowing what the Church clearly states is a sin can help, and knowing what's a near-occasion of sin is also significant for recovery. But it can take time and assistance to learn to release the worry that a fall into sexual compulsion is lurking around every corner and instead learn to trust God and rely on his grace. If we fear whatever is around the corner or feel prematurely guilty for it, it makes it a whole lot easier for there to actually *be* something around that corner when there wasn't before.

5. Dreams

This one is difficult because it's a gateway drug that we don't choose, but it's one of the most common questions I get. When we have a sexual dream, it's tempting to let it be a springboard either into engaging a compulsion *or* into a scrupulous moment that we addressed above. Neither option is healthy in the long run for obvious reasons.

First, it's helpful to understand that sexual dreams are completely natural occurrences. This is hard to believe when they mimic content we've viewed or behaviors we've engaged in, or if they involve people we know or attractions we don't usually have in real life. Many times it also feels as if we're actually "in control" or lucid in our dreams, making the feeling that we're committing a sin even more believable. Even when these things are the case, we are *not* guilty for what occurs in our sexual dreams.

In his *Summa Theologiae*, St. Thomas Aquinas addressed sexual dreams, or what he called "nocturnal pollutions" (hands-down the best name for them, in my opinion). He gives several reasons why these dreams occur and answers whether they're sinful—including them happening as a result of lustful thoughts throughout the day or even excessive eating and drinking, or purely as an attack from the devil. Whatever the case, our reason is impaired in sleep, leading Aquinas to conclude, "Hence it is manifest that nocturnal pollution is never a sin, but is sometimes the result of a previous sin."[7] If we're guilty of excessive eating or drinking or of lustful thoughts throughout the day, we're still guilty of those when they cause a sexual dream, but we're not guilty for the dream itself.

One helpful comparison I make when speaking to women about sexual dreams is between a sexual dream and one that involves violence. We do weird things like punch, kick, or even shoot people in our dreams when we wouldn't react that way in real life. Are we guilty for those actions? Chances are, you'd answer probably not, and the same goes for sexual actions in our dreams. However, if we allow our sexual dreams to spur us on—by fantasizing about the content, masturbating, or engaging in some other compulsion—then we're clearly guilty of a sin. If we are engaging in an action while we're aware that we're awake, it's a sin, but if we're sleeping and unaware, then our reason is still impaired and sin isn't occurring.

On the flip side, having a sexual dream can cause scrupulosity and guilt, which poses the danger of falling into an ashamed and scrupulous cycle like we discussed above. When you have a sexual dream, it's important to find a balance. Do your best to wake up, acknowledge that it happened and how your body reacted, and try to move forward without guilt or engaging in what the dream offered any further. Praying a quick prayer of protection can be helpful, or even just treating the dream with a sense of lightheartedness by shrugging it off, no matter how disturbing it was.

Especially if you're in recovery and noticing improvement, sexual dreams can certainly be a tactic of the enemy to make you believe you're still in a pattern that you're not. If you're noticing your sexual dreams increasing even though your unwanted sexual behaviors and thoughts throughout the day are steadily decreasing, it might be the enemy. Simple things like praying before bed or responding lightheartedly to his attempts can help sexual dreams remain just natural occurrences that literally happen to *everyone*— and not a weapon against you.

Conclusion

Identifying gateway drugs can feel meticulous or as if we're being overdramatic, but I promise they're worth examining. If one of them that I've listed above caused you to feel defensive, I invite you to look at that particular gateway drug more closely. Sometimes we get defensive because we know that we're keeping something around—or taking advantage of something—that we know we shouldn't. If the thought of getting rid of or perhaps changing your interactions with certain things like social media and scrupulosity feels anxiety-inducing or as if you're taking away something you "need," then that's all the more reason to make a change. Addiction is a beast, and it will try to find any path to get back into your life to claim it again—so cut it off at the roots.

9
THE PRACTICALS

If I should fall even a thousand times a day,
a thousand times, with peaceful repentance,
I will say immediately, "nunc coepi" (now I
begin).

–Venerable Bruno Lanteri

Despite my insistence that I cannot write a self-help book and that the practical aspects of recovery aren't a replacement for the deep work of interior healing, there are several things that can help a woman kickstart the recovery process. These tips are also gathered from my own recovery journey and from watching the recoveries of dozens of other women. They vary from ideas that are fairly fundamental to the process to things that might just be helpful for some.

Wherever you are in your recovery journey, the first principle is that you can't recover without doing *anything*. This is why I ask that initial question to anyone who talks to me about recovery: "What are you willing to do?" We aren't our own saving grace, but we're definitely asked to at least *participate* with grace. The ways we women can participate with that grace can look similar to that of men, in some ways, and other methods are uniquely feminine. One of the most practical things you can do for your recovery is to not compare your journey to anyone else's, particularly that of men. What motivates and heals the masculine heart can look very different from what motivates and heals women, and those differences are not something we should ignore when reflecting on our own stories or accompanying others in their healing. The most important aspect is that you put your best effort into these practicals and allow others to help you—but none of that can happen if you don't begin.

1. Learn Your Triggers

A trigger is something that causes us to seek relief in a sexual compulsion. Triggers can come in all shapes and sizes, whether it's a location, emotion, sound, or situation. Learning your triggers is, again, a very individual process, and it can also be incredibly detailed. Most of us don't have just one trigger that sends us down the path of seeking out pornography, masturbation, or some other release. Understanding each trigger and having preventative measures in place for when they occur is a helpful place to begin in the recovery journey.

Start by having an attitude of nonjudgmental curiosity about what your triggers are, remembering that just because one arrives doesn't mean you have to give in—being triggered isn't a sin. Observe the workings of your mind, heart, and body throughout your day, and notice moments where you feel a strong need to engage in whatever unwanted sexual behavior you struggle with. Is it when you're tired and haven't had enough sleep? Is it when you have a stressful exam or conversation coming up? Is it when you're bored, angry, or anxious, or after you've been drinking alcohol? Or maybe when your head hits the pillow at night or you're alone in your room on your phone? There's no such thing as a stupid trigger, and each one is worth paying attention to, no matter how insignificant it may seem.

In our recovery small groups, our ministry trains women to identify their triggers early on in the support process. It's important, though, that identifying our triggers *leads* somewhere. We don't identify triggers just so that we can let them dictate us, now with our awareness. It's about naming them so we can acknowledge our experiences and discover appropriate responses. Ignoring triggers or letting them control us are the two extremes that keep an addiction running.

Part of why it's crucial to explore the nuances of your triggers is so that you can find other ways to respond to yourself or your surroundings in a manner that actually *meets your needs*. In our support groups, we have women construct something called a "Freedom Plan," where they list their triggers in different categories: emotions, situations, and locations; then they write three other activities to do in response to each particular trigger instead of giving into a sexual urge. These activities should directly correlate with the trigger—a version of "let the punishment fit the crime," so to speak.

For instance, if your trigger is loneliness (which is perhaps one of the most common I've heard cited by the women I work with), it probably won't be helpful to go on a run. Instead, recognize that you're seeking a filler for your loneliness in pornography, masturbation, or fantasizing. Find something to truly fill the need of your heart, whether that's calling a friend or loved one, grabbing a cup of coffee with someone you enjoy, or taking time for intentional conversation with Jesus through journaling. (See, there are three!) Our triggers become far less powerful when we allow them to tell us something that we need and respond in a healthy way, rather than being a threatening presence that controls us.

2. Seek Accountability

Accountability, I believe, is essentially a necessity for long-term recovery. I waited too long to entrust my story and struggles to friends and ask for their help. But once I did, I experienced the power of being accountable to others. On a surface level, knowing that you need to answer to a friend or someone else you trust when you fall can definitely be preventative. But on a deeper level, accountability is a beautiful way to cultivate the love in friendship that is such medicine to our souls.

If you don't already have an accountability partner, asking someone whom you've felt comfortable disclosing to is a great place to start. (No, your therapist or spiritual director doesn't count!) Ask yourself which person you would call if, for instance, you lost your job or someone you love was in the hospital—the person who has your back in whatever curveball life throws at you. That person is a great place to start for accountability.

One of the most frequent situations that I hear from women when it comes to accountability is the accountability relationship "fizzling out." Usually this happens because there weren't clear expectations set on the front end when the relationship was established. It's helpful to plan with your accountability partner for how often you'll check in and what those check-ins will look like. And once you've taken time to explore your triggers, sharing those triggers and the habits you want to try in response is also helpful. This sets a standard or goal that the relationship is supposed to meet. And knowing each other's triggers and helpful habits (if both of you are trying to recover and heal) gives you material to offer one another in tough moments. Having a set spiritual practice, such as a daily prayer or weekly sacrifice you offer for each other, can also strengthen the accountability relationship.

Group settings, as we've already discussed, are also particularly powerful for women. Because our hearts are often so relationship-oriented—though in incredibly unique ways—having a group setting where relationships grow and thrive because of struggling and healing together as an intentional community is a game changer for many women. Finding a small group through a ministry like the one I run, or joining a local twelve-step group, is an intimidating and challenging step, but the benefits are often worth the effort.

Consider using filtering or accountability software—such as CovenantEyes or Qustodio—with your accountability partner or support group as well. Software isn't perfect, and if it's your only practical tool, it may not get you very far in recovery. But as a supplement to other things, especially a solid accountability relationship, software can greatly enhance how we communicate with others trying to help us along the road to recovery.

3. Ditch the Smartphone

At the risk of sounding like a Luddite, I think getting rid of your smartphone can be one of the best decisions you can make for yourself in recovery, if you're struggling with consuming pornography specifically. I mentioned this earlier, but to me, a porn addict having a smartphone in their back pocket is comparable to an alcoholic keeping a beer in their back pocket—except in the case of the alcoholic, there aren't a billion reasons per day to take the beer of your pocket and look at it. A smartphone constantly reminds you that it's there (yes, even when it's on silent), so much so that scientists are now researching the possibility of "screen addiction."[1]

I find that when I pose to women the possibility of getting rid of a smartphone, they typically begin telling me the reasons why they can't. I get it; I did something similar—and a smartphone would certainly be most convenient. However, it's worth examining if the reasons you might be coming up with in your head right now to keep your smartphone are about requirement or *preference*. It's okay to prefer a smartphone, but is it actually *required* of you? Even if your job requires it, consider getting a secondary "dumb" phone that you can use when you leave work or on the weekends. However much it may seem like it, very few people actually have to conform to having a smartphone with them at all times. Many companies have developed minimalist phones to help combat screen addiction, such as the LightPhone II (my personal favorite) or Wisephone. Leaving the opportunity for temptation locked in your desk, even if it's just for the weekend, is well worth the hassle.

There's something to be said about allowing, or even choosing, inconvenience, recovery aside. It's undoubtedly easiest to have a smartphone, especially as our world conforms more and more to it. Businesses assume you have one—hence menus, parking meters, and event tickets with QR codes and links. Deciding to allow inconvenience, for the sake of something or someone, is a way to emphasize that particular thing or person's value. For whatever reason, it's worth altering your typical way of life for. Being free from pornography is worth the inconvenience of living without a smartphone, or at the very least living with a heavily restricted one. Whatever the excuse you have is, it's probably just that—an excuse. There's a way to work around it; you just have to be willing to do so.

4. Take Care of Your Body

There's a ton of evidence piling up that exercise is good for keeping up not just your physical health but your mental health as well, with a minimal commitment to exercise yielding amazing results in cases of people suffering from immune or mood disorders. Some mental disorders, such as anxiety and depression, can be linked to sexual compulsion; ADHD and bipolar disorder in particular have a high co-occurrence rate among sex addicts.[2]

Sexual compulsion and sin aren't just affronts to the dignity of others—particularly if you're using others while engaging in these behaviors. They are affronts to your own dignity, including that of your body. Exercise is a way of both dignifying and disciplining your body; it shows you the value of keeping your body healthy while also training you in active resistance to your flesh. If you're not currently exercising, even minimally, as part of your recovery, I highly recommend finding at least a small amount of time each day for it. It doesn't need to be a power hour in the gym; it just needs to be a method that you find personally challenging, and it should feel as if it's *costing* you, not necessarily wrecking you. Depending on your current health, state in life, and how much fitness is a part of your life, this method varies.

I often hear fasting recommended to men trying to recover in the Church, and I think it most certainly has a place, but perhaps with a few caveats. In my experience, another common co-occurring struggle with sexual addiction in women is that of body image. Often but definitely not always, women who are struggling with sexual sin are also feeling high levels of insecurity about their weight, appearance, or exterior expression of femininity. This is a complexity that deserves its own book, but for now, it at least is pertinent regarding fasting. Fasting in recovery for some women could go one of two ways: first, it could become an unhealthy outlet for disordered eating habits; second, it could turn the focus too much onto self-denial and take necessary attention away from fulfilling their needs in healthy, uplifting ways.

Fasting is an incredible spiritual discipline, but when you're caught up in the extreme of constantly indulging in your desires and compulsions, it's not helpful to swing the pendulum to the opposite extreme. Denying yourself genuine comforts in food while also trying to cut out the comfort you've been finding in sexual behaviors may just dig you a deeper hole. Instead, try to incorporate small fasts—denying your desires in small ways, such as giving up alcohol or sweets for a period of time, or consider offering a small fast for your accountability partner's recovery or intentions for extra motivation. If you find that it yields fruit, consider increasing the practice or just committing to a consistency with it. If you're also struggling with body image, fasting is probably not the best approach in recovery. First, the focus should be placed on eating *healthy* and *well*, which when you're suffering from an eating disorder in particular, is often far more difficult than denying yourself. Giving your body necessary nutrition gives your brain the fuel it needs to function, and you want your mind firing from all cylinders while trying to recover. The more depleted you are in your body, the more difficult it will be to respond productively and compassionately to the impulses of your mind.

We certainly need to deny our flesh, but we also need to work to restore our understanding of the dignity of our bodies. It's not one or the other; as is often the case in Catholicism, it's a "both-and." We cannot treat our bodies as prisons for our souls, only getting in our way and meant to be denied. There have been heresies that tried that method, and it didn't work out too well for them. Instead, we need to come from a place of reverence for the purpose of the body and treat our bodies well accordingly while also incorporating disciplines that truly shape us into women who are healthy and whole.

5. Track Your Cycle

Another topic that deserves its own book: holistic, theologically informed cycle education for young women. The menstrual cycle and the hormones that come along with it play a massive role in how women interact with day-to-day life and sexual temptation, and yet most of us received very little information or formation on the topic within the Church. The connection between the menstrual cycle and sexual temptation was mind-blowing to me when I finally heard it discussed in college, and tracking my cycle only confirmed it. Practicing basic fertility awareness isn't just good for understanding your health as a woman in general—some doctors are beginning to refer to it as women's "fifth vital sign"— but it's also a game changer when it comes to identifying patterns of sexual temptation, sin, and compulsion.

It becomes pretty straightforward (when it's finally pointed out): the main hormones at play in a woman's body are estrogen, progesterone, and a smaller amount of testosterone. During the menstrual cycle, the hormone levels rise and fall; estrogen levels peak around ovulation, while progesterone peaks right after ovulation (and during pregnancy)—low levels of both can create more mood swings and irritability, such as right before a period. Increased estrogen affects sexual desire and arousal, while increased progesterone decreases it. Put simply: when you're ovulating, your sexual desire and ease of arousal spike. This doesn't mean you don't experience desire or arousal any other time of the month; it just means that perhaps you're more susceptible than usual when ovulating because of a natural reoccurring reality in your body.

Men don't experience the same ups and downs in hormones that we do as women. If you have a relationship with or interact with men in any capacity in your daily life, you probably have clear evidence of this. The menstrual cycle is a unique part of a woman's sex drive, so it makes perfect sense that it's also a unique part of a woman's sexual struggles. Your cycle remains a silent killer in the area of sexual sin and compulsion *until* you're aware of it; then it becomes another tool for a healthy recovery.

There are multiple ways to begin tracking your cycle, whether it's through a fertility awareness method—such as the Creighton Model, the Marquette Method, or the Sympto-Thermal Method—or even just beginning with a basic app (though don't let an app be a reason to hold onto your smartphone!). Simply tracking your period, symptoms, and mood changes over a few months can give you a pretty good idea of what's happening to your hormone levels throughout your cycle. Try to take note of an increase or decrease in sexual temptation or compulsion along with it. I know plenty of women who *only* struggle with pornography and masturbation during ovulation, experiencing very little temptation other times of the month. This doesn't excuse behavior, but it makes it more understandable—their hormone levels have naturally increased their sex drive, and part of their recovery is finding healthy ways to take care of themselves during ovulation and placing proper protections in place for when temptations arise.

Tracking your cycle is one of the best ways you can take care of your body as a woman and a surefire way to identify how your hormones might be affecting your recovery. Communicating whether your cycle affects your triggers to your accountability partner also gives them notice—that way, they can increase their support during times of the month that are tougher for you.

6. Take Note of What You're Watching or Fantasizing About

This was not a concept I always believed in, but I've seen it be fruitful over and over again. If you're consuming pornography or engaging in sexual fantasies in particular, *don't* ignore the content of what you're consuming or imagining. Our attractions and what we find appealing or arousing are not random. Often it's part of a neural pathway that was previously paved by another experience or emotion.

For instance, consuming male-dominant violent pornography as a woman can often be linked to childhood trauma, including experiences of sexual abuse at the hands of men. Consuming female-on-female pornography can have links to an absent or abusive mother or female figure. The links aren't unilateral or intrinsic, but the content we're consuming or fantasizing about *does* reveal something about us, whether it's something as serious as childhood trauma or a deeper emotion that we've been ignoring. Knowing the holes that you're trying to fill or emotions you're trying to control or mitigate (i.e., your triggers) is powerful, but so is knowing what you're trying to fill or control *with*. What provides that false sense of satiation or control you're looking for? The answer doesn't need to be something to fear, but rather it can reveal a place where we need to receive the Lord's healing and compassion.

7. Pray, Pray, Pray

As I've already covered, you cannot simply pray addiction away. I think this is one of the most harmful attitudes regarding this issue and many others that got accidentally communicated sometimes through the Church. However, while our sexual issues deserve physical and psychological struggle, they also need our spiritual attention.

Developing an interior life in the midst of sexual addiction or sin is brutal and can make you feel like a total traitor, but it's also the beginning of our relief when we allow it to be. You cannot recover without the grace of God, and you cannot experience the grace of God without giving him the space and time to give it to you. Creating a daily prayer routine and participating in the sacramental life of the Church doesn't "fix" an addiction, but it reminds you to consistently place yourself in the presence of God and receive his love and mercy.

Don't just pray about your sexual sin, though that's important too. Pray about your life, your desires, your needs—and *listen* to Jesus. His voice is sometimes so incredibly quiet, to the point of feeling silent, but he speaks, and he wants you to hear him. Particularly for women, it's crucial that we be vulnerable with Jesus and leave time and space to converse with him, heart to heart.

A friend was just telling me some wise words she heard from a priest who works in deliverance ministry: "Women often need to learn to sit and *feel* with Jesus—to allow themselves to work through their feelings, no matter how extreme or uncomfortable, in the presence of the Lord. *Then* they can break agreements or cast out influences from the enemy." It's simple but so true, and not something that's encouraged for women enough. I'm a pretty hard *T* ("thinker") on the Myers-Briggs personality typology, which means I primarily make decisions and interact with others by thought, and I can articulate those thoughts pretty easily. My feelings are a different story. This, however, doesn't mean that I—or other women like me—don't have emotions that we need to process and truly feel. Often it actually means that our feelings can sneak up on us because they're so strong yet not our main mode of deciding or interacting. Whether you're a woman with her heart on her sleeve or a tried-and-true stoic (or somewhere in between), you need to be given permission to feel, especially in the presence of God. There's so much in the depths of our minds and hearts that only he knows and that only he can speak into.

If I could say there's one thing that's been at the center of my healing and recovery from pornography—and my journey toward heaven in general—it's that I fell in love with Jesus Christ. In the scraps of time and attention I gave him, so much less than he deserves, he took hold of my heart and didn't let it go. So much of my long-term recovery hasn't been about a white-knuckled control or prevention of sexual compulsion; it's been about feeling his tenderness reach places that desperately needed reaching and his voice calling me on to better and more beautiful things. There's a powerful quote from Fr. Joseph Whelan, a Jesuit priest:

> Nothing is more practical than finding God, than falling in Love in a quite absolute, final way. What you are in love with, what seizes your imagination, will affect everything. It will decide what will get you out of bed in the morning, what you do with your evenings, how you spend your weekends, what you read, whom you know, what breaks your heart, and what amazes you with joy and gratitude. Fall in love, stay in love, and it will decide everything.[3]

There you have it, folks. There's nothing more truly practical than finding God, falling in love, and giving him your life. While you can't *just* pray addiction away, addiction won't go away without praying—not to mention, your life won't be as beautiful, peaceful, and full as it can be without prayer.

You don't need to become an instant contemplative in order to begin developing an interior life, and what works for someone else may not be the way you best communicate with the Lord. Prayer doesn't have to be pristine and perfect to be effective. As we've already discussed, it's often in the messiness that we finally hear him clearly. Patterns of sexual sin and compulsion often leave your feminine heart fluctuating between two extremes of total numbness and an overwhelming weight that feels almost impossible to bear. Go before him, in your numbness or that crushing weight, and pray. It decides everything.

Accountability is fundamental, knowing triggers is necessary, and taking care of your body and practicing fertility awareness are crucial. But knowing and falling in love with Jesus is the beginning and end of our lifelong healing. Nothing works completely without the infusion of his grace.

10
RESTORING IMAGINATION

We seek an enlargement of our being. We want to be more than ourselves. . . . We want to see with other eyes, to imagine with other imaginations, to feel with other hearts, as well as with our own. . . . We demand windows.

–C. S. Lewis

The Trap of Fantasy

Almost a decade ago, a team of researchers based at the University of Texas and the University of Notre Dame conducted a study on female sexual fantasies, surveying 355 female college students. The findings were quite disturbing (once again, the methods of these studies often involve unethical materials and means): about 62 percent of women regularly fantasized about forced or violent sex with both men and women.[1]

Our imagination is a wild place; it can be the bedrock of creativity and innovation but also clearly the source of some pretty messed up stuff. However, whatever our sexual fantasies are involving—whether it's dominance and violence or just erotic romantic experiences—it's often easier to pardon ourselves for an image in our minds than it is for consuming pornography or masturbating. Often women in my small groups have shared that when it comes to the latter two, they *know* when they've fallen, but with fantasy it's hard to find the line.

It took me quite some time to recognize that sexually fantasizing in my mind was the equivalent of finding porn online. It wasn't "better" because I left my computer or phone out of it; it wasn't more "dignified" because it didn't involve watching other real people. Fantasizing is incredibly harmful not just because it *does* actually involve objectifying others without their knowledge or consent but also because it easily convinces us it's completely acceptable and doesn't harm anyone.

For clarity, there's a big difference between a sexual thought or image coming to your mind (especially about someone you're physically attracted to or in a relationship with) and *entertaining* that thought. Initial thoughts entering our mind are not sins, but choosing to allow a suggestive thought to remain and develop in our mind is. Again, these thoughts *do* harm people—it harms the person or people you're fantasizing about because it's a very secretive form of using them, and it harms you by doing damage to the gift of your imagination.

Women's fantasy lives in particular are strong, in the sexual realm and beyond. While men's overall fantasies tend more frequently and consistently toward sex, women's fantasies vary from sex to romance to career to just fantasy about everyday life. The female capacity for fantasy has become more and more dominated by sexual imagery and opportunity, though, as our oversexualized culture continues to expose us to more content. To make matters more confusing, many psychologists, doctors, and other experts in their field have been advising women to *engage* in regular sexual fantasy to increase their libidos and assert their needs in their sexual relationships (not that violent dominance, a common fantasy for women as cited above, makes for much of a healthy sexual relationship). One "sexologist" wrote in a piece for the *Huffington Post* that "other than our skin, our brains are the biggest sex organ we have. We are supposed to use them. We are supposed to have an active fantasy life. Sexual fantasies do not make us sluts. Nor do they suggest that we have trouble in our current relationship. Fantasies make us healthy sexual beings."[2] The author goes so far as to assert that if we *don't* fantasize, our sex lives as women are not complete. Fantasizing is deeply encouraged—not just by sexologists—and branded as "healthy" and even necessary when communicating with a spouse.

Within marriage, it's worth clarifying the difference between fantasy and memory, and communicating about sex for the sake of your marriage versus using your spouse for your own pleasure. First, when you have a sexual relationship with your spouse, it's not a sinful act to recall a memory of your experiences with them out of love or gratitude, as long as recalling is not for your own individual pleasure or arousal. Second, it's absolutely necessary and healthy to communicate about your sex life but to do so for the sake of increasing unity and charity with each other. For a woman in particular, because of changes in libido, to suggest an idea that could enhance the mutual experience of spouses is vastly different than a husband or wife treating their spouse as a tool to fulfill their "active fantasy life." Further, fantasizing about or suggesting violent or otherwise disordered or degrading sexual acts, even with a spouse, is never acceptable. Contrary to popular sexologist belief, we do not get a free pass on our sexual fantasy life, even—or perhaps especially—when we're married. In fact, you're only *more* responsible for protecting the dignity of your spouse and the sacredness of your sexual life together because of the Sacrament of Marriage.

I have found in my own life and work that, much to my initial surprise, sexual fantasy can be a harder habit to break than pornography or masturbation. I've seen many women enter a long period of sobriety from porn or masturbation, only to be leveled by the capability of their fantasy lives. Sometimes this is because they didn't take note of their ongoing fantasies while they were caught up in other sexual compulsions. Other times, they discover it as a new outlet for those compulsions once porn, masturbation, or other sexual acts are no longer a part of their daily life. Whatever the case, recovering from fantasy requires a restoration of our relationship to reality and a cultivation of a holy imagination.

Fantasy versus Reality

For Catholics, reality isn't something to be messed with or ignored. Our relationship to reality ultimately has a lot to do with our relationship to truth. In living and abiding in reality, we recognize that we are not the determiners of truth; rather, Truth is a person infinitely more powerful than us, and he invites us to discover him more and more deeply. The philosopher Jean Bethke Elshtain, in an introduction she wrote to Luigi Giussani's *The Religious Sense*, said the following about reality:

> We lose this world [of beauty and power] in an age of ideology as we manipulate, fabricate, and strive to master reality. We overvalue our own schemes. We forget that there is a world we are invited to know—to know, and yes, to love . . . the person is one who engages, seeks, works, yearns, loves. We come to know the world and others precisely because we are drawn out of ourselves and toward an object outside ourselves. We move toward a reality we did not make.[3]

In order for us to receive God's presence to us, we *must* exist in reality. As Psalms 118:24 says, "This is the day the LORD has made." Reality, which we are not in control of or sovereign over, is ordained and created by God to lead us ultimately toward him. Different theologians have expressed in unique ways that heaven isn't ethereal or fantasy-like but rather *real* to its core.[4] It's a never-ending participation in the glorious reality of God.

Elshtain says further that one must "love the truth more than yourself."[5] As she articulated beautifully, we're called as Christians to *love* reality, to love the truth, more than ourselves or anything we desire. This determines our relationship to our everyday life, whether full of joy or suffering. If we can love what God provides and allows more than ourselves because we truly desire him first, we've arrived at sanctity.

This is why living in fantasy, whether or not it's sexual, can never be conducive to a life of holiness. Fantasy is saying no to the day the Lord has made and wanting to live in the one *we've* created instead—meaning we assume it's somehow better. I'm not talking about having daydreams or desires; a good mental check on daydreams that was recommended to me is that if your constant daydreaming leaves you with dissatisfaction or sadness about your life, then you've left the realm of true reality and entered into your own. We're called to "in all circumstances give thanks" (1 Thes 5:18) or to "rejoice in it and be glad" (Ps 118:24) with what God has given us, not to constantly be looking for life elsewhere.

Sexual fantasy is a "no" to reality, in the sphere of our sexuality. Again, there's nothing wrong with sexual desires or even fulfilling some of them in the context of marriage. But just as in every other area of our lives, we have to first be present to God in the reality of our sexuality *as it is*, particularly when it comes to our state in life. Our sexuality and sexual experiences must be rooted in the truth of what God is inviting us into, not in what we want. Human desire is powerful, but it's also flippant and easily disordered; it can't be the determinant of what's truly good for us. Reality, as God has made or allowed it, is what's *always* good for us. As Communion and Liberation—the lay movement of which Giussani is the founder—summarizes: "Reality has never betrayed me."[6]

Reorienting toward Reality

If you're caught in a life of fantasy, chances are you've noticed it affecting other areas of your life. Maybe it's manifesting as a shorter attention span, brain fog, or the inability to truly focus and be present in your daily life. Fantasy conditions us to seek life outside of where our life truly is, whether sexually or otherwise. Maybe, above all else, fantasy has just created a deep sense of dissatisfaction in you—that's what it's aimed toward. It makes us believe that the fullness of life is always somewhere else than exactly where we are.

In order for the pattern of fantasy to end, you have to cultivate a *gratitude* for the reality that's in front of you. For me and the other women I've accompanied, fantasizing doesn't end when you've "finally gotten a grip" on lust or "taken control" of your mind. It ends when you begin to learn that reality is worth living in because *Jesus is there*. Our imagination is actually meant to be at the service of reality, not in opposition to it. If we're finding the foundation of our creativity and imagination in the reality of God, our minds are able to expand and discover the true, good, and beautiful even more deeply than before—knowing that, in the end, it's all a reflection of him. The imagination, when subject to reality, is a tool for contemplation, not destruction.

Weeds and Wheat

In recovery, especially when trying to recover from sexual fantasizing, do not try to find your freedom in crushing your imagination. It's not evil or sinful in itself, and the fact that fantasy has been a sinful habit or compulsion of yours only means that your mind is capable of great things. Freedom from fantasy comes in setting our imagination, creativity, and memory on the beauty of God, not avoiding or hiding from the life of our mind. A scripture professor of mine in grad school once illustrated a helpful concept through the parable of the weeds and the wheat in the Gospel of Matthew. Jesus tells the story of servants who are eager to pull out weeds that are growing among the wheat. Their master instead tells them to wait and let the weeds grow with the wheat until harvest (Mt 13:24–43). My professor told us simply, "Jesus is telling us that putting our sole focus on the flaws doesn't actually advance us in the life of sanctity. Growth of the wheat makes the weeds obvious. . . . Jesus is telling us, 'Grow,' and that he'll *show* us what needs to be weeded out in time."

Focusing on the growth of virtue doesn't take away responsibility for our vices, but it does place our energies and motivations in a much more productive place. Venerable Fulton J. Sheen said that "the Christian ideal is always positive rather than negative," reiterating that our interior life is more about yes than no. Ultimately we're focused on being magnanimous—or "great-souled"—not just people who avoid wrongdoing.

People who are magnanimous do not ignore reality; they participate in it and see it as the place to meet God's will and grow in holiness. Holding on to fantasy and seeing it as a "less severe" outlet for sexual compulsion or lust will be detrimental not only to long-term recovery but also to this growth in magnanimity and the life of your soul.

There are a couple of steps to staying grounded in reality and fostering imagination from that foundation. First, we need to practice what 2 Corinthians 10:5 recommends: "Take every thought captive in obedience to Christ." Our thoughts, especially habitual ones, can feel as if they overpower the rest of our mind. It's easy to feel swept up in a moment of fantasy before you've even realized it's begun. When beginning to tackle a habit of fantasizing, learning to examine your thoughts at their origin is key. As soon as you catch yourself having a sexual thought, have a simple go-to question that allows you to take that thought captive. Ask something like, "Is this glorifying God?" or "Is this helping me become a healthier person?" or "Is this honoring me or the person I'm thinking about?" These questions aren't to cause you guilt but rather to allow a pause before continuing with the thought and redirecting the powers of your mind toward the truth.

Another helpful tactic that a woman in recovery gave me, when I was struggling to overcome fantasy, was to first create a mental picture of an adoration chapel or church that I particularly loved. She told me to etch the monstrance or tabernacle as clearly as possible in my mind and to hold that image close. When I caught myself in a moment of fantasy, she encouraged me to snap my fingers—mentally, if not sometimes literally—and recall that image, intentionally placing my mind in the act of recalling the presence of Christ. It may sound silly or too simple, but I've found it's incredibly effective. It's another form of taking thoughts captive without engaging in excessive guilt or anxiety. Plus, it doesn't shut down the creative aspect of my mind but rather uses it to give God a moment of time that I may not have given otherwise.

Using the creativity of our minds is the second key part to re-grounding in reality. As I said before, we need to say yes to true creativity, rooted in reality, instead of just saying no to fantasy. The imagination is a powerful tool, and it can be a source of deep joy in the service of God. It shouldn't be shut down out of fear or guilt. When trying to recover from fantasy, place a great deal of focus on filling your mind with the good, true, and beautiful, and giving it intentional moments to engage in creativity.

Reading can be a wonderful way to begin, but read *good* books, not just the pithy stuff. Incorporate ten minutes of spiritual reading into your prayer life or set a goal for reading one good novel a month. Part of why fantasy can be so difficult is because our minds can be incredibly active. So put your mind toward something productive and fruitful. Many people make excuses that they don't have "time" to read. Friend, if you have time to fantasize, you have time to read. Keep a book in your purse or backpack and pull it out in moments when you might fantasize out of boredom. Keep one by your bed and read yourself to sleep (instead of scrolling on your phone!). If you don't know where to begin when it comes to reading, I've included a list of different spiritual, psychological, and even fictional suggestions in the appendix of this book.

Replacing the things that can so easily feed our dissociation with reality—such as scrolling endlessly through social media or binge-watching Netflix—with fruitful things that give our mind something good to truly chew on is also helpful. Consider substituting whatever you're currently watching with an engaging podcast or audiobook. One of my friends, who's beautifully committed to staying grounded in reality, shared with me that she was listening to *The Lord of the Rings* on audio while learning to knit and how she was feeling so much peace from replacing binge-watching with this habit. It's the perfect example of how filling our time with good content, as well as allowing our minds to engage in creativity, is actually *more restful* than escaping through fantasy or other habits that cause a disconnect with reality.

There are many other ways to let creativity flow from a place of being rooted in the truth of reality. In recovery, dedicating yourself to learning something new that allows your imagination and creativity to thrive—such as knitting like my friend, playing an instrument, or learning one of the various mediums of art—can turn a small way of saying yes to reality into a massive bolster for long-term recovery, particularly from fantasy. When our mind is filled with and dedicated to the true, good, and beautiful, it becomes much easier to say no to what isn't of God.

When Fantasy Takes Over Prayer

Another strikingly honest question I get from women is how to handle images from a fantasy coming to distract them during prayer. Occasionally those thoughts can even take on a spiritual tone, suggesting disturbing thoughts about Our Lord, the saints, or other holy things they might be trying to focus on during prayer. One woman told me that prayer is actually where these thoughts plague her the *most*, making her more and more avoidant of prayer.

To put it quite simply, that's exactly the point. If you notice the images from fantasy coming up in prayer, especially aggressively to the point where it feels absolutely exhausting—or even impossible—to get away from them, it's almost always a tactic of the enemy. He doesn't just do this to women who are recovering from sexual sin; he does it to *everyone*. God allows these moments to increase our strength in mental prayer.

A helpful distinction, when working through this struggle with mental prayer, is between what's *fantasy* and what's *distraction*. Thomas Merton clarifies this for us:

> The kind of distractions that holy people most fear are generally the most harmless of all. But sometimes pious men and women torture themselves at meditation because they imagine they are "consenting" to the phantasms of a lewd and somewhat idiotic burlesque that is being fabricated in their imagination without their being able to do a thing to stop it. The chief reason why they suffer is that their hopeless efforts to put a stop to this parade of images generate a nervous tension which only makes everything a hundred times worse.[7]

Fantasy and distraction, particularly in prayer, are distinguished by the will. Fantasy engages our will, not just our thoughts or imagination, while distraction can go on in the mind without the will's consent. As Merton says,

> The mind and memory and imagination only work, in meditation, in order to bring your will into the presence of its object, which is God . . . consequently the mind and memory and imagination have no real job to do. The will is busy and they are unemployed. So, after a while, the doors of your subconscious mind fall ajar and all sorts of curious figures begin to come waltzing about on the scene. If you are wise you will not pay any attention to these things: remain in simple attention to God and keep your will peacefully directed to Him in simple desire, while the intermittent shadows of this annoying movie go about in the remote background. If you are aware of them at all it is only to realize that you refuse them.[8]

What Merton prescribes for distraction is to focus on the will rather than trying to control the mind. As he points out, we can make ourselves incredibly tense and even *more* distracted—not to mention ashamed—when we dedicate our energy in prayer to suppress the images that come into our imagination during prayer.

Especially when these thoughts are particularly sexual or disturbing, it can easily feel as if they're a result of your sin or compulsion. Remember, fantasies are sexual thoughts and images that you *consent* to, not just ones that pop into your mind randomly—even if those random thoughts mimic content you've taken in or fantasized about. That's why it's crucial to focus our attention on keeping our will in a posture of desiring God. No fruit is lost in prayer when this is our goal. In fact, it can prove even *more* fruitful to spend time in prayer where we're constantly redirecting our will from distraction than if we never tried at all.

I encourage you, if you're in recovery, to not rely on mental prayer alone. What I mean by this is to supplement your prayer life with some supportive resources that can help facilitate or ground your meditative prayer. When your mind feels easily hijacked, it's helpful to have some content to already be chewing on or open prayer with. Again, spiritual reading is wonderful, as well as reading and meditating on scripture. The practice of *lectio divina* can be particularly redemptive since it engages the imagination in reflection on God's Word. Praying the Rosary and meditating on the mysteries of Christ's life have a similar effect. Music can also be a beautiful way to lead your soul toward God's presence. These things aren't meant to make up our prayer life but rather to be a springboard for deeper mental prayer and ultimately contemplation.

Confession and Imagination

Venerable Fulton J. Sheen once said, "Nothing in human experience is as efficacious in curing the memory and imagination as confession—it cleanses us of guilt and, if we follow the admonitions of Our Lord, we shall put completely out of our mind our confessed sins."[9] Confession, as we've already discussed, can be one of the most terrifying places for you to go as a woman struggling with sexual sin. But Sheen is right—if you want true freedom for your mind, you must confess the things that have been plaguing it.

In doing so, you can come into sharing the mindset that Jesus has about your sin—that it's at the bottom of the ocean floor or cast completely from him. Psalm 103:12 reminds us that "as far as the east is from the west, so far has he removed our sins from us"(Ps 103:12). We believe, as Catholics, that when you walk out of the confessional, you have truly been made new. Nothing resets the mind quite like this. If the enemy comes back to taunt you with something you've previously seen, done, or fantasized about that you've since confessed, you can take comfort in the fact that Jesus doesn't remember it, so you no longer have to either.

Reality Won't Betray You

There are many things that cause us to want to escape—anxiety, stress, depression, boredom—and fantasy is an easy, built-in method of doing so. Re-grounding yourself in reality and allowing your imagination to flow from it means allowing these emotions and experiences that encourage us to escape to come to the surface. Depending on how uncomfortable or extreme they are, this can also be a time when seeking out professional help can be deeply reassuring. I found that my own habit of fantasy often stemmed from moments of anxiety. I felt the symptoms of my anxiety most potently in the morning when I first woke up and faced the day, and again at night when I laid down with no distractions. When do you think I found myself fantasizing? You guessed it—when I first woke up in the morning and when my head hit the pillow at night.

But like many chapters of this book have already attested to, there's a greater freedom that comes from being present to the uncomfortable, tense, frightening, and difficult emotions and experiences we have, rather than escaping from them. As long as our tactic is escaping through fantasy, we'll stay in a trap. But reality, as Giussani says, will truly never betray us. It may be painful and difficult to live in at times—excruciating even—but it's also the place where we find our deepest joy, peace, and union with God that's possible in this life.

11
RECAPTURING INNOCENCE

Because children have abounding vitality, because they are in spirit fierce and free, therefore they want things repeated and unchanged. They always say, "Do it again"; and the grown-up person does it again until he is nearly dead. For grown-up people are not strong enough to exult in monotony. But perhaps God is strong enough to exult in monotony. It is possible that God says every morning, "Do it again" to the sun; and every evening, "Do it again" to the moon. It may not be automatic necessity that makes all daisies alike; it may be that God makes every daisy separately, but has never got tired of making them. It may be that He has the eternal appetite of infancy; for we have sinned and grown old, and our Father is younger than we.

–G. K. Chesterton

I feel a certain hesitancy as I approach this chapter on innocence, since this is a concept that hits close to home for so many of the women I've spoken and walked with. It hits close to home for me, and it might be the hardest lesson I'm still exploring. It requires a lifelong rehabilitation, much like the other parts of our hearts damaged by sexual sin. But there's a certain tenderness to innocence that's painful to speak of, especially when we feel it's been hopelessly lost.

There's a recurring theme of hatred toward childhood that comes up in my ministry, and I've noticed it in my own self throughout the years, particularly in recovery. When sexual sin and trauma are a part of your history, it's hard not to hate that history. I also think hating your childhood is a lot easier than facing that feeling that your innocence is permanently lost or was taken from you.

Growing up, I always wanted to be older than I was. When I was in middle school, I wanted to be in high school, and in high school, I wanted to be in college . . . so on and so forth. My family jokes often about the different memories of me scrambling to keep up with my older siblings or how I practically groveled to go to school full-time in kindergarten, like them. Part of this is just my personality—I tend to push myself well past my limits—but looking back, it always felt like if I was just older, I would finally be comfortable with myself or fulfilled in a way I wasn't at whatever time.

This all caught up to me when I was completing my graduate degree in theology right after college. I had graduated college early, and I completed my master's degree in a year. While I don't regret the educational path I took, it hit me how much I'd pushed myself when I was hitting a breaking point a few months before graduation from my master's program at twenty-two. Why had I pushed so hard, and what had it gotten me? Just a quicker path to adulthood, and I had never found the fulfillment I was looking for the whole time.

Discomfort with Innocence

My consistent desire to be older, coupled with my unwanted experiences and exposure to and subsequent addiction to pornography, was a recipe for me being uncomfortable with being a child. Innocence either felt strange or out of reach. Still, to this day, if you want to insult me, tell me I'm too young to understand or do something. I've found that the visceral reaction I have to being childlike, youthful, or innocent isn't isolated to my experience but actually a common thread among many women who have struggled with sexual sin and compulsion. It manifests in different ways for each one of us, but it's there. There's a discomfort with, if not a hatred for, innocence. One woman articulated it to me as "wanting to leave my childhood self behind as quickly as possible—I *hated* her."

When you're experiencing this discomfort or hatred of childhood and innocence, you first have to examine the roots of it and where it might have begun. If you're a victim of some form of trauma or abuse—even if it doesn't seem grave to you—that can easily create a thread of this repulsion toward innocence. The feeling of having your innocence taken or even robbed from you is incredibly painful to reconcile. It feels easier to propel forward and try to leave the moment—or moments—of trauma or abuse behind, finding safety in adulthood. There's a sense in children that adults have power and the ability to defend themselves, which is the opposite of what you feel as a victim of trauma and abuse, whether it happens as a child *or* as an adult.

Often if trauma or abuse is a part of your story, hating your childhood or childhood self can also be a form of releasing anger that's meant for those involved in or the perpetrators of your abuse and trauma. It's much easier, for many reasons, to blame or take our anger out on ourselves than on those who have hurt us. Antonieta Rico, from the Army Resilience Directorate, explains how our own reaction to our abuse and trauma is what leads to self-blame:

> A person's reaction to a threat or traumatic event
> involves complex factors, including subcortical (uncon-
> scious) processes of the brain. Besides fight or flee, shut-
> ting down is also a common defensive brain response
> to threat. But, because people expect a "fight or flight"
> response, when a person does neither people question
> whether an assault occurred. Survivors themselves
> may not understand their own responses, leading to
> self-blame.[1]

Self-blame is a painful reality that most victims of abuse or trauma experience, precisely because of the reaction detailed above.
"Shutting down," "going into autopilot," or "numbing out" are
common responses to abuse or trauma, and it can be confusing
and agonizing to look back and wonder why we reacted the way we
did. This can be compounded if you shared about your experiences
and were met with more blame or even written off.

Self-blame also applies to our exposure to pornography or masturbation. We can look back, especially if we were children when it
happened, and wonder why we didn't stop ourselves from watching, reading, or acting—or why we didn't stop those who were
introducing these things to us. Why did we go back for more when
the first instance was so traumatizing? First, because the content or
action we discovered caused a release of dopamine in our brains,
leaving us physiologically wanting more. And second, because we
were trying to make sense of an experience that left us feeling out
of control, whether positively or negatively. Especially for a child,
first exposures feel especially strange and leave you feeling powerless
because there's a lack of psychosexual development.

Whatever your story is and wherever your self-blame might be
coming from, if it's manifesting as a hatred toward your childhood
or a despair at innocence, this can be a painful part of recovery. I
may sound like a broken record, but it bears repeating: it's not just
okay but beneficial to seek help to resolve these results of wounding. Whether it's with a therapist or trusted spiritual director,

having a guide as you unpack the sorrows and joys of your story can be a game changer. You don't have to go it alone.

Self-blame—when it comes to trauma, abuse, and/or subsequent sexual addiction (not all sexual addictions come from a significant moment of trauma or abuse)—leaves us feeling as if our childhood was wasted, twisted, or even a lie. Innocence can feel like a taunting joke, a phantasm that haunts us with a promise of what we could've had but gave away or lost. Once again, I'm feeling a hesitancy as I try to step into this. It's so delicate and tender, and yet so key to our long-term recovery and overall confidence in our identity as daughters of God.

The nightmares that resulted from my unwanted experiences as a child were often centered on an older man whom I admired or felt safe with. It was a pattern I only identified when I was a teenager: I would feel safe or comfortable with a man, perhaps a father figure, teacher, or family friend, and would subsequently have a nightmare in which I was being abused by them. None of the men I ever had a nightmare about actually did anything *close* to abusing me; it was just a patterned reaction to feeling safe. Why this pattern happened is still somewhat a mystery to me, but the message it sent me was simple: "You cannot be safe with men. Fatherhood is dangerous. Being a child is dangerous." Daughterhood was not a part of my identity that I felt comfortable with because it meant being in a state of trust or reception. It's worth noting that my earthly father is an incredible man who has provided an example of faith and fidelity to me and my family. My story is evidence that complex psychosexual and sexual wounds can occur in your life, even with grounded and amazing parents. The pattern of these nightmares didn't resolve until I went through that summer of therapy after graduating college, in which I was finally able to process those unwanted experiences and find deeper healing.

Whether it's through sexual or psychosexual wounding, perhaps the message your heart received is the same: childhood is not safe. *Daughterhood* is not safe. Adulthood, however, is—so rush forward and don't look back. Innocence either resulted in damage, fear, or shame; it's a gift that others got to have, but you feel you either had it ripped from you or gave it away. This is not the truth, but it can certainly feel like it. However deep that feeling might be, restoring innocence is possible.

Learning to Be a Child

Forgiveness

In order to start restoring innocence, you have to first be *okay* with being a child in the presence of the Lord. You don't necessarily need to *love* it (so many of us don't, whether or not we're in recovery!), just to start learning comfortability with the posture of being a child. Often this means removing blame from our childhood selves before anything else.

One of the most rewarding activities we have women in our small groups take part in is called the "Forgiveness Letter." In the activity, the women are asked to take a generous time of quiet and write a letter to themselves, beginning from a foundational wound, trauma, exposure, or experience that they can see is aggravating their current struggle, and working their way through different instances up to the present. At each step, they forgive themselves, whether it's for freezing during an abusive experience, for returning after their first exposure to pornography, or for believing lies that were sold to them through their experiences. A therapist can professionally guide someone through processing their trauma in ways that no one else can, and this activity is no replacement for that guidance. But in a spiritual sense, forgiving ourselves can help us at least release any bondage we might have to our adverse experiences and help us let go of any anger or animosity we have toward ourselves as children.

After they write the letter, we recommend the women take intentional time, preferably in the presence of the Blessed Sacrament, to read the letter to themselves. There's something about reading it back that really hits home. Many women give us the feedback that of all the activities we have throughout our small-group curriculum, this is the most healing. Writing down our experiences and forgiving from the perspective of an adult gives a new lens that helps us see how young and vulnerable we truly were in the midst of them. So many of us would never direct the blame and anger toward someone else's child, a younger sibling, or our own child the way we do to ourselves in our younger years. Recognizing the blame and anger for what it is—a reaction and response to a place where we've been hurt and don't feel safe, and therefore are looking for a form of control—helps us begin the process of letting our innocence be restored.

Forgiving ourselves doesn't mean the blame of all these moments *actually* belongs on us, though for our sins it does. Forgiving ourselves is necessary not because of actual fault but because we've been holding a grudge, whether reasonably or not. Forgiving is the only way to let go of that blame, both reasonable and unreasonable alike.

Dependence

As I've already mentioned, the pervasive thought when trying to recover innocence isn't actually that all is lost but that childlike innocence isn't *safe*. For whatever reason, it can feel as if our innocence got us into trouble in the past and is best avoided now.

In order to recover the innocence we long for, we have to abandon ourselves *completely* to God. This can be a long and slow process at times, something that must begin over and over again. Every human being inherently fears abandonment, at least at first. It feels like the total opposite of safety to completely surrender ourselves to someone else. But when that someone is God, there's nothing safer. Sometimes the hardest thing to surrender completely to God is the attachment we have to guilt. It's easy to believe that our sin is "too much" for God or that his mercy only extends to certain areas of our lives. Despite perhaps *feeling* like humility, this mindset, deep down, is actually rooted in our own pride. If I think I have the ability to surpass the reaches of God's grace in my sin, that's still a way of believing I'm more powerful than he is. St. Teresa of Avila summarized this in her *Way of Perfection*: "In my opinion, the devil would like us to believe that we possess humility and, if he could, he would like to cause us, in exchange, to lose all confidence in God."[2]

True childlike dependence is *actually* humble and only increases our confidence in God's mercy and protection, and as a result, it increases our peace. Dependence doesn't mean we ignore our sin and fake innocence; rather, it means that we recognize God's love as the source of our *renewal* in innocence. But he cannot renew us if we don't depend on him. Spiritual writer Fr. Jean C. J. D'Elbee also spoke of the danger of allowing our sin to come between us and our dependence on Jesus:

> Never let your past sins be an obstacle between you and Jesus. It is a ruse of the devil to keep putting our sins before our eyes in order to make them like a screen between the Savior and us. Think of your past sins for your own humiliation, or to persuade yourself once again of your weakness, of your unworthiness; think of them in order to find happiness in expiation, in order to confirm your firm resolution not to fall again— certainly that is necessary—but especially in order to bless Jesus for having pardoned you, for having purified you, for having cast all your sins to the bottom of the sea. . . . Do not go looking for them at the bottom of the sea! He has wiped them out; He has forgotten them.[3]

One of the beauties of innocence is a recognition that we don't have to take care of everything ourselves. Children depend on their parents quite literally for their whole livelihood. Part of the abrupt loss of innocence, along with self-blame that tells us what happened to us is all our fault, is the feeling that *fixing* it is all our responsibility. It's easy to believe this about our sinfulness, but as so many of the saints have articulated, believing that will only prevent us from receiving the salvation God longs to provide for us. Dependence and the repeated surrender it requires allows us to humbly accept this unfathomable gift from our Father who loves us.

Something that still blows my mind to think about, and that I still struggle to accept, is that God is merciful not *in spite of* our sin but *because* of it. We think of our sin as an obstacle that God must overcome or overlook in order to love us and have mercy on us. Depending on the gravity of the sin in question, we think that means all the more work on the part of God. The opposite is true. When we depend on God's mercy in our sinfulness and submit ourselves to him with humble confidence, God is actually delighted and completely undeterred. St. Thérèse of Lisieux even goes so far as to say our sin attracts God's mercy to us.[4] She's not the only one. St. Augustine beautifully wrote the phrase *miseri cor dare*—"God gives his heart to the miserable." It's from this phrase that we derive the word *misericordia*, which means "mercy." We can depend on God's mercy because he is offering his very heart, not begrudgingly looking past our sin.

Joy

Perhaps the most necessary and most difficult aspect of innocence to recover is that of joy. Joy is *really hard* to experience and live from as an adult. The weight of the world—not to mention the weight of our sin and experiences surrounding us—is enough to rob us of it. But joy is attainable for us by the grace of God, no matter our circumstances. Children experience joy because of their ability to take delight in things *as they are*. They're not distracted by the same things we are. Their attention can remain undiverted and absolutely enraptured by whatever might be in front of them.

I've had the privilege of nannying for several families throughout my college and young adult years, and I've watched with fascination over and over as children discover the simplest of things and accept all sorts of circumstances (except for when they really *don't* accept things and let you know!). Maybe we can't experience the world around us and our own circumstances for the first time in the same way a child can, but in a way, we can. If we've allowed our experiences and sinfulness to prevent us from living in joy, we *can* rediscover that way of life—we can live it fully for the very first time.

Just like forgiveness and dependence, joy doesn't mean that we ignore our sexual sin and woundedness. In fact, joy actually comes from *accepting them as they are*, recognizing God's presence and intentionality remaining with us even in the midst of pain. It can feel impossible at first to look at our sin and brokenness and allow it to become a source of joy for us instead of one of deep sorrow and shame. But when we do, we make immense spiritual progress, beyond what we can fathom.

St. Thérèse of Lisieux, who was named a Doctor of the Church for her spirituality of the "Little Way," made this incredibly clear, essentially putting into words and practice being childlike before God. Referring to the arms of Jesus as an "elevator" to heaven, she writes,

> The elevator which must raise me to the heavens is Your arms, O Jesus! For that I do not need to grow; on the contrary, I must necessarily remain small, become smaller and smaller. O my God, You have surpassed what I expected, and I want to sing your mercies.[5]

St. Thérèse isn't being presumptive, saying that it's fine if she continues in sinful patterns because God will love her anyway. She's recognizing where any grace, merit, or sanctity comes from: Jesus. Our greatest cause for joy can be that if we trust Jesus enough to constantly submit ourselves to him and allow ourselves to be carried by him, there is only one place he will bring us. We can be joyful because of an unshakable confidence that we are *loved*, no matter what, and that there's a Father who is always waiting with open arms when we fall short. It's a freeing place to live from—so few of us ever truly do it.

Looking Forward

A guest I had on a podcast episode beautifully spoke of her need to be "re-parented" after her experiences growing up. She spoke of how in mental prayer, she encountered Mary and Joseph, and the Holy Family as a whole, as they welcomed her in and allowed her to be a child with them. Her imagery struck me in its simplicity but also in its hopefulness. One thing she said in particular will probably always stay with me: "I don't think I could have had a more beautiful childhood than the one I have with the Holy Family now."

In summary, and reflecting on my friend's profound words, perhaps recovering innocence isn't so much about rectifying all that happened to us as children and "taking something back" but rather allowing something new to be given to us in the present. We will probably never understand all the events of our lives and their subsequent wounds on this side of heaven, but what we *can* know is this "new childhood." Experiencing this is what allowed my friend to recount her past, and the wounds that came with it, without an ounce of regret. When we become like children in the arms of the Father *now*, it stops mattering whether we've always been—or gotten to be—that way. What matters most and brings us the deepest joy is that he intended us to be innocent with him now.

12

THE WHITE HORSE

Now I know who I am, and now I may be who I am, for my love loves me, my love has bestowed trust on me.

—Hans Urs von Balthasar

Your Love Is Meant to Change the World

When I had just entered recovery in college, I had the privilege of being in a semester-long course on Pope St. John Paul II's *Theology of the Body* as part of my studies for my major. The timing was certainly providential. There I was, finally repeatedly saying no to porn and ready to take in the truth about sexuality and the human person with fresh eyes. The professor was a wise, tenderhearted man who knew the work like the back of his hand. His gentle eloquence while speaking about sex, the body, and other topics that had become so tainted for me was absolute medicine to my soul.

He preferred to conduct his exams face-to-face, and I went into my final hesitatingly. Once I had answered only one question, my professor surprised me by telling me I had passed and asking me if I had any questions of my own for him. Perhaps I had a few that were more curriculum-based—if I did, I can't remember—but without really realizing it, I began to tell him about my history with pornography.

"I am just beginning to heal from an addiction to pornography, and I'm afraid I've . . . ruined something. That I could never be married, or never be whole in my sexuality in the way John Paul II talks about, the way you've talked about . . ." I remember looking down at my hands the whole time I was speaking. My professor looked away and paused for a long time, and I felt incredibly awkward, until he finally spoke.

"No," he said with his gentle smile. "Lust did not attack you because you cannot love. Lust attacked you because your love is meant to change the world."

His words deeply affected and honored me at the time, but they take on more significance each time I repeat them or reflect on them. He was generous enough to give them to me. It's a message I believe was meant not just for me but for every woman—and man—whom I have the privilege to encounter in my life and work now. They give me the hope that perhaps it's actually true: "Where sin increased, grace overflowed all the more" (Rom 5:20). The very place of your deepest sin and struggle is the very place God has called you to imitate him, to win souls for him. I've seen it time and time again—lust does not come for the numb, apathetic souls who have already given into defeat. It comes for the passionate, the tender, the zealous, the sacrificial, and those qualities, by the grace of God, are what are victorious in the end.

If you've been reading this book hoping to find any solace, let it be those words from my dear professor. Because of the indescribable mercy of our God, your sin does not ruin you if you allow him to save you. Instead, it becomes the very catalyst for your sanctity. Saints like Mary Magdalene and Augustine are the perfect examples of this. Their wide-reaching, shocking sinfulness was only an indication of how much *power* was in them. Jesus can identify that. He sees that it's that very capacity for grave sin that also means they have the capacity for great virtue. As he said himself, it's the lukewarm that give him a particular kind of heartache (see

Revelation 3:16). When that power and capacity are harnessed by a God who's absolutely strong and relentless . . . it's unstoppable, and it paves our path to heaven.

To illustrate what I'm talking about, I'm going to take you back to *The Great Divorce*. If you remember the first part of the story of the ghost with the red lizard, you might be happy to know that his story doesn't end with the red lizard simply being ripped from his shoulders. Lewis uses the next part of the narrative to explain precisely this concept: that God doesn't just take our sin from us and heal us. He uses it to transform us into someone entirely different. He doesn't just dispense with the old man for the sake of the new. The old is the very tool he uses to chisel out the new in us.

Once the ghost finally allows the angel to kill the red lizard, Lewis's main character watches in astonishment as something radical happens:

> For a moment I could make out nothing distinctly. Then I saw, between me and the nearest bush, unmistakably solid but growing every moment solider, the upper arm and the shoulder of a man. Then, brighter still and stronger, the legs and hands. The neck and golden head materialised while I watched, and if my attention had not wavered I should have seen the actual completing of a man—an immense man, naked, not much smaller than the Angel. What distracted me was the fact that at the same moment something seemed to be happening to the Lizard. At first I thought the operation had failed. So far from dying, the creature was still struggling and even growing bigger as it struggled. And as it grew it changed. Its hinder parts grew rounder. The tail, still flickering, became a tail of hair that flickered between huge and glossy buttocks. Suddenly I started back, rubbing my eyes. What stood before me was the greatest stallion I have ever seen, silvery white but with mane and tail of gold. It was smooth and shining, rippled with swells of flesh and muscle, whinneying and

stamping with its hoofs. At each stamp the land shook
and the trees dindled.

The new-made man turned and clapped the new
horse's neck. It nosed his bright body. Horse and master
breathed each into the other's nostrils. The man turned
from it, flung himself at the feet of the Burning One,
and embraced them. When he rose I thought his face
shone with tears, but it may have been only the liquid
love and brightness (one cannot distinguish them in
that country) which flowed from him. I had not long
to think about it. In joyous haste the young man leaped
upon the horse's back. Turning in his seat he waved a
farewell, then nudged the stallion with his heels. They
were off before I well knew what was happening. There
was riding if you like! I came out as quickly as I could
from among the bushes to follow them with my eyes;
but already they were only like a shooting star far off
on the green plain, and soon among the foothills of the
mountains. Then, still like a star, I saw them winding
up, scaling what seemed impossible steeps, and quicker
every moment, till near the dim brow of the landscape,
so high that I must strain my neck to see them, they
vanished, bright themselves, into the rose-brightness of
that everlasting morning.[1]

My heart feels so full every time I read this passage that I'm stum-
bling over how to unpack what's written here. Lewis is describing
how radical God's mercy on and love for us is. The ghost, when
freed from his bondage to sin, becomes truly himself. In turn, the
red lizard, who was once the sin that kept the ghost in chains and
prevented him from entering heaven, when surrendered to the
power of God and killed, becomes a white horse—the very means
by which the man can now enter paradise.

Reflecting on this passage is currently the conclusion of our
small-group curriculum in the ministry I work for. While not all
women are in recovery by the time the group ends, many of them
are, and listening to each of them, regardless of where they are

in recovery, share how they've seen God's goodness working in the midst of something they previously saw as only broken and shameful is always profound to me. In response to the question "What is your white horse?" I've heard women share newfound intimacy with Christ, a deeper regard for their own dignity, or a new step in pursuit of their vocation, among many other beautiful victories. Many of them cry—I love how Lewis calls it "liquid love" in the passage above—and marvel at how God is transforming their sin into something glorious, something that can be a major part of their individual path to sanctity. They can see after journeying in vulnerability and healing with a community, at least a little more clearly, that their love was meant to change the world and that's why lust has been such a cross for them. They were meant to enjoy the fullness of love in heaven, and the enemy has spared no effort in trying to prevent them from getting there—but he hasn't won. I've seen him defeated over and over again.

I almost always cry in these concluding sessions, too, because in looking at each woman I see my own white horse. No matter what their story might hold—each one is so unique—I see an unbelievable generosity from the heart of God in that I *get* to hear these stories and journey with these women. Out of the place in myself that I only perceived as dark, irredeemable, and disgusting has come the opportunity to love and be inspired by countless women. I have the chance to receive them in their loneliness, shame, apathy, fear, and strife, and hold their hands while they let Our Lord into those wounds and heal. I get to see the very transformation he's been working mercifully in me happen in others, and even more beautifully, time and time again. People ask me why I'm not scared to speak so boldly about sinfulness, especially sexual sin, and I believe this is why: without speaking up, without my own brokenness, I would not get to see him act in such a profoundly tangible and beautiful way. I know the women whom I work alongside in our organization feel similarly. For us, it's a glimpse of eternity.

What's Next?

Women who are in recovery and experiencing the peace that can only come from God's healing hand often find themselves—not in a bad way but rather the "stuck" you feel after an event you've prepared for or looked forward to is over, or after you've overcome an immense challenge. I think of Samwise Gamgee at the end of *The Return of the King* looking around him and his peaceful home—after literally being at the center of the seeming end and then renewing the world—and simply saying, "Well, I'm back." Entering recovery can feel like that. It seems like the great battle and struggle are over, and we're just "back" to normal life.

The question "What do I do now?" is one I'm familiar with in my own story and one that I've seen asked repeatedly by other women in recovery. It feels wrong to sweep such a long, exhausting, rewarding process under the rug and pretend it never happened, especially when there's so much need just for the topic to be covered in the first place, and you know that many women might be out there struggling silently like you. I think the answer is simple. Find *your* white horse. Not everyone is called to public ministry, but that doesn't mean the work of art God wants to make out of your addiction is any less powerful. He will continue to work wonders both privately and perhaps even publicly in you and through you, if you pay attention.

Recovering love is a lifelong process and one that reaches far beyond the realm of addiction and recovery. There's a whole world out there of broken people in need of the healing touch of Jesus Christ, and perhaps recovering addicts are one of the best examples of what it means to receive that touch. Your white horse, your specific call to sanctity, will very specifically ask you to be a testament to what can happen when you relinquish your red lizard. Everyone has one—or several. The difference between most people and addicts is that addicts at least *know* they have a red lizard wrapped around their shoulders. So *say something* about yours, whether it's just with family and friends or a wider community. I think we are in an age that is in desperate need of hope—of stories that are deeply human and make people realize they're not as isolated as they want to believe.

As my husband regularly tells me, "The human heart never changes." It will *always* desire eternal beatitude, union with its Creator, and it will either strive to fulfill that desire in him or in the most pathetic and horrible of places. I feel that maybe I sound like a broken record because I've been trying to say it in so many different ways, but the problem isn't just porn addiction, or masturbation, or sexual fantasy. The problem is that the human heart is in deep need of rescuing and too few allow themselves to be rescued. Too few go on the journey of recovering the love that they're destined for.

Me? I'm still recovering, every day, and I'm guessing you are too—from whatever sins we momentarily decided were a better fulfillment of our desire than him. But such is the journey on this side of heaven. We're still returning, still learning to hear his invitation to go back to the beginning. *The Great Divorce* has one final note of hope for those of us who are still pilgrims here. On the Man and White Horse's way into heaven, a song breaks out:

> The Master says to our master, Come up. Share my rest and splendour till all natures that were your enemies become slaves to dance before you and backs for you to ride, and firmness for your feet to rest on.

> From beyond all place and time, out of the very Place, authority will be given you: the strengths that once opposed your will shall be obedient fire in your blood and heavenly thunder in your voice.

> Overcome us that, so overcome, we may be ourselves: we desire the beginning of your reign as we desire dawn and dew, wetness at the birth of light.[2]

"The strengths that once opposed your will shall be obedient fire in your blood and heavenly thunder in your voice": There are few things quite as hopeful as that. Your ensnarement in lust can become your impetus to love . . . a love that can change the world, even while you're in the process of learning how to love in the first place. An addiction—the very thing that can make you feel so controlled and imprisoned—when surrendered to God can become "firmness for your feet to rest on." If you just surrender, just let yourself be overcome.

I've searched my heart and mind for a conclusion to this book, and perhaps the fact that I can't find one is precisely the conclusion it needs. In recovery and healing, there is no conclusion—not here. I'm still learning to receive the Love that truly changes the world, to be a vessel of it, to let it change *me* first. It takes repeatedly waking up, being radically honest over and over again, diving deeper into relationship, and wearing my face. It takes a growing knowledge of the practical and spiritual, the compromises and distrust that keep me from living in reality and childlike dependence. Most of all, it takes a recognition that leaving behind addiction isn't about recovery *from* something but recovery *of* something: the Love that I was always meant to belong to—the One you're meant to belong to, too.

RECOMMENDED READING

For more on pornography, addiction, and healing:

Be Restored by Bob Schuchts

Unwanted: How Sexual Brokenness Reveals Our Way to Healing by Jay Stringer

Uncompromising Purity by Kelsey Skoch

The Porn Myth by Matt Fradd

Dopamine Nation by Anna Lembke

Addiction and Grace by Gerald May

For spiritual growth:

Searching for and Maintaining Peace by Jacques Phillippe

I Believe in Love by Jean C. J. D'Elbee

Learning the Virtues by Romano Guardini

The Interior Castle by St. Teresa of Avila

This Tremendous Lover by Eugene Boylan

The Return of the Prodigal Son by Henri Nouwen

The Dialogues by St. Catherine of Siena

The Fire Within by Thomas Dubay

Introduction to the Devout Life by St. Francis de Sales

No Man Is an Island by Thomas Merton
The Heart of Perfection by Colleen Carroll Campbell

For restorative fiction:

Persuasion by Jane Austen
Emma by Jane Austen
Kristin Lavransdatter by Sigrid Undset
Till We Have Faces by C. S. Lewis
Jayber Crow by Wendell Berry
The Lighthouse by Michael O'Brien
Brideshead Revisited by Evelyn Waugh
The *Father Brown* Mysteries by G. K. Chesterton
The Lord of the Rings Trilogy by J. R. R. Tolkien

NOTES

1. The Beginning

1. *The Missal: Containing All the Masses for Sundays and for Holy Days of Obligation*, ed. John P. O'Connell and Jex Martin (Chicago: Catholic Press, 1955).

2. William Gurnall, *Daily Readings from the Christian in Complete Armour*, ed. James S. Bell (Chicago: Moody Publishers, 2015), January 11 entry.

3. Joseph Ratzinger, "The Feeling of Things, the Contemplation of Beauty," message to the Communion and Liberation meeting at Rimini, August 24–30, 2022.

4. Alice von Hildebrand, *The Privilege of Being a Woman* (Ypsilanti, MI: Veritas Press, 2002), xiii.

5. Edith Stein, "The Separate Vocations of Man and Woman," in *Essays on Woman* (Washington, DC: ICS Publications, 1996), 75.

6. Fyodor Dostoyevsky, *The Brothers Karamazov*, trans. Richard Pevear and Larissa Volokhonsky (New York: Alfred A. Knopf, 1880).

7. Jay Stringer, *Unwanted: How Brokenness Reveals Our Way to Healing* (Colorado Springs, CO: Nav Press, 2018), xx.

8. Bob Schuchts, *Be Restored: Healing Our Sexual Wounds through Jesus' Merciful Love* (Notre Dame, IN: Ave Maria Press, 2021), 15.

9. *Merriam-Webster*, s.v. "pornography," accessed October 12, 2022, https://www.merriam-webster.com/dictionary/pornography.

10. Gerald May, *Addiction and Grace: Love and Spirituality in the Healing of Addictions* (New York: HarperOne, 1988), 24.

11. May, *Addiction and Grace*, 25–31.

12. Lacy Bentley, "Gender and Childhood Pornography Exposure: New Research Reveals Surprises!" Defend Young Minds, September 29, 2016, https://www.defendyoungminds.com.

2. The Problem with Purity Culture

1. *ST* II-II, Q. 157, A. 1.

2. Heather Rupp and Kim Wallen, "Sex Differences in Response to Visual Sexual Stimuli: A Review," *Archives of Sexual Behavior* 37, no. 2 (2009): 206–18.

3. Rupp and Wallen, "Sex Differences in Response to Visual Sexual Stimuli," 211.

4. Rubén Alarcón, Javier De La Iglesia, Nerea M. Casado Espada, and Angel Luis Montejo, "Online Porn Addiction: What We Know and What We Don't–A Systematic Review," *Journal of Clinical Medicine* 8, no 91 (January 2019), doi.org/10.3390/jcm8010091.

5. Audrey Assad, "Personal Witness," recorded at SEEK 2015 conference, Soundcloud recording, March 3, 2015, audio, 45:40, https://soundcloud.com/udreyssad/personal-witness.

6. *ST* I-I, Q. 1, A. 8.

3. How We Got Here: The History of the Pornography Industry

1. Joe Duncan, "The History of Pornography: From the Paleolithic to Pornhub," Medium.com, May 31, 2019, https://medium.com/unusual-universe/the-history-of-pornography-from-the-paleolithic-to-pornhub-4123dbeef37e.

2. Duncan, "The History of Pornography."

3. "The Brothels of Pompeii," Pompeii Tours, May 12, 2022. https://www.pompeiitours.it/attractions/brothels-of-pompeii/.

4. John Clarke, review of *The Archaeology of Sex, Love, and Gender in Pompeii*, by Lourdes Conde Feitosa, *Bryn Mawr Classical Review* (2014), https://bmcr.brynmawr.edu/2014/2014.03.43/.

5. "Facts about Human Trafficking in the US," DeliverFund, April 17, 2020, https://deliverfund.org/facts-about-human -trafficking-in-the-us/.

6. "How Porn Fuels Sex Trafficking," Fight the New Drug, July 14, 2021, YouTube video, 4:40, https://fightthenewdrug.org/ how-porn-fuels-sex-trafficking-video/.

7. Duncan, "The History of Pornography."

8. Carrie Gress, *The Anti-Mary Exposed: Rescuing the Culture from Toxic Femininity* (Charlotte, NC: TAN Books, 2019).

9. See Betty Friedan's quote: "A woman is handicapped by her sex, and handicaps society, either by slavishly copying the pattern of man's advance in the professions, or by refusing to compete with man at all." *The Feminine Mystique* (New York: W. W. Norton, 1963), 509.

10. Peggy Orenstein, *Girls and Sex: Navigating the Complicated New Landscape* (New York: Harper, 2016), 34. (Author's note: Orenstein raises thought-provoking questions and identifies many problem spots surrounding the conversation of sex and sexuality with young women, but I do not recommend her work from an ethical standpoint.)

11. Orenstein, *Girls and Sex*, 34.

4. Waking Up

1. *Sexaholics Anonymous* (Simi Valley, CA: SA Literature, 1989).

2. Jay Stringer, *Unwanted: How Brokenness Reveals Our Way to Healing* (Colorado Springs, CO: Nav Press, 2018), 35.

3. Stringer, *Unwanted*, 11.

4. C. S. Lewis, *The Great Divorce* (New York: HarperCollins, 1946), 108–9.

5. Lewis, *The Great Divorce,* 109–10.

6. Pierre Teilhard de Chardin, "Patient Trust," IgnatianSpirit-uality.com, May 21, 2022, https://www.ignatianspirituality.com/prayer-of-theilhard-de-chardin/.

5. Radical Honesty

1. Anna Lembke, *Dopamine Nation: Finding Balance in the Age of Indulgence* (New York: Dutton, 2021), 176.

2. Lembke, *Dopamine Nation*, 184.

3. Henri J. M. Nouwen, *Can You Drink the Cup?* (Notre Dame, IN: Ave Maria Press, 1996), 97.

6. Recovering Relationship

1. *ST* II–II, Q. 153, A. 5.

2. Lembke, *Dopamine Nation*, 139.

3. C. S. Lewis, *The Four Loves* (New York: Mariner Books, 1960), 122.

4. Lewis, *Four Loves,* 37.

5. Lewis, *Four Loves*, 37.

6. 1 Thessalonians 5:16–18: "Rejoice always. Pray without ceasing. In all circumstances give thanks, for this is the will of God for you in Christ Jesus."

7. Lewis, *Four Loves*, 65.

8. Lewis, *Four Loves*, 66.

9. Lewis, *Four Loves*, 91.

10. Lewis, *Four Loves*, 94.

11. Lewis, *Four Loves*, 114.

12. Lewis, *Four Loves*, 121.

7. Wearing Your Face

1. C. S. Lewis, *Till We Have Faces* (New York: Mariner Books, 1956), 294.

2. Hans Urs von Balthasar, *Heart of the World* (San Francisco: Ignatius Press, 1979), 138.

3. C. S. Lewis, *Prince Caspian* (New York: HarperCollins, 1951), 218.

8. The Gateway Drugs

1. Jaron Lanier, *Ten Arguments for Deleting Your Social Media Accounts Right Now* (New York: Henry Holt, 2018), 5.

2. *The Social Dilemma*, directed by Jeff Orlowski (Los Gatos, CA: Netflix, 2020).

3. Alex Hern, "Netflix's Biggest Competitor? Sleep," *Guardian*, April 18, 2017, https://www.theguardian.com/technology/2017/apr/18/netflix-competitor-sleep-uber-facebook.

4. Aldous Huxley, *Brave New World* (New York: HarperCollins, 2006), 40.

5. Lanier, *Ten Arguments*, 26.

6. Ignatius of Loyola, *The Spiritual Exercises* (Charlotte, NC: TAN Books, 1999), 220.

7. *ST* II–II, Q. 154, A. 5.

9. The Practicals

1. Raquel Lozano-Blasco, Pilar Latorre-Martinez, and Alejandra Cortes-Pascual, "Screen Addicts: A Meta-Analysis of Internet Addiction in Adolescence," *Children and Youth Services Review* 135 (April 2022).

2. Richard Blankenship and Mark Laaser, "Sexual Addiction and ADHD: Is There a Connection?" *Sexual Addiction and Compulsivity* 11, nos. 1–2 (January 2004): 7–20.

3. Joseph Whelan, "Fall in Love," in *Finding God in All Things: A Marquette Prayer Book* (Milwaukee: Marquette University Press, 2009). (Author's note: This passage is often also attributed to Fr. Pedro Arrupe, SJ.)

10. Restoring Imagination

1. Raj Persaud and Dr. Jenny Bivona, "Women's Sexual Fantasies: The Latest Scientific Research," *Psychology Today*, August 28, 2015, https://www.psychologytoday.com/us/blog/slightly-blighty/201508/womens-sexual-fantasies-the-latest-scientific-research.

2. Logan Levkoff, "Sexual Fantasies: Why Women's Sex Lives Aren't Complete Without Them," *Huffington Post*, last updated March 6, 2012, https://www.huffpost.com/entry/sexual-fantasies-women-sex-lives_b_1185108.

3. Jean Bethke Elshtain, foreword to *The Religious Sense*, by Luigi Giussani (Montreal: McGill-Queen's University Press, 1997), xi.

4. See, specifically, Joseph Ratzinger's *Eschatology*, and C. S. Lewis's essay "The Grand Miracle" in *God and the Dock* for discussions on this. Joseph Ratzinger, *Eschatology: Death and Eternal Life*, trans. Michael Waldstein, 2nd ed. (Washington, DC: The Catholic University of America Press, 1988); C. S. Lewis, "Miracles," in *God in the Dock*, ed. Trustees of the Estate of C. S. Lewis (Grand Rapids, MI: Eerdmans, 1970).

5. Elshtain, foreword to *The Religious Sense*, xi.

6. Davide Perillo, "Reality Does Not Betray," *Communion and Liberation*, February 1, 2017, https://english.clonline.org/news/current-events/2017/02/01/reality-does-not-betray.

7. Thomas Merton, *New Seeds of Contemplation* (New York: New Direction Books, 1961), 222–23.

8. Merton, *New Seeds of Contemplation*, 222.

9. Fulton J. Sheen, *From the Angel's Blackboard: The Best of Fulton J. Sheen* (Liguori, MO: Liguori Publications, 1996), 147.

11. Recapturing Innocence

1. Antonieta Rico, "It Really Wasn't Your Fault: How Understanding the Brain's Response to Trauma Can Lessen Victim-Blaming and Self-Blame," U.S. Army, December 10, 2020, https://www.army.mil/article/241611/it_really_wasnt_your_fault_how_understanding_the_brains_response_to_trauma_can_lessen_victim_blaming_and_self_blame.

2. Teresa of Avila, *The Way of Perfection*, trans. Kieran Kavanaugh (Washington, DC: ICS Publications, 2000), 47.

3. Jean C. J. D'Elbee, *I Believe in Love: A Personal Retreat Based on the Teaching of St. Therese of Lisieux* (Manchester, NH: Sophia Institute Press, 2001), 12–13.

4. Thérèse of Lisieux, *Story of a Soul*, 3rd ed. (Washington, DC: ICS Publications, 1975), 200.

5. Thérèse of Lisieux, *Story of a Soul*, 208.

12. The White Horse

1. C. S. Lewis, *The Great Divorce* (New York: HarperCollins, 1946), 113.

2. Lewis, *Great Divorce*, 113.

Rachael Killackey is the founder and executive director of Magdala Ministries, which helps women find hope and healing from sexual addiction.

She earned bachelor's and master's degrees in theology from Ave Maria University and is pursuing a certification in sex addiction therapy from MidAmerica Nazarene University. She previously worked as the assistant director of faith formation for catechesis for the Diocese of Nashville.

Killackey has been a guest on various podcasts, including *Lust is Boring* with Jason Evert, *Pints with Aquinas* with Matt Fradd, *The Covenant Eyes Podcast*, *Wide Open Spaces*, *Wellness Wednesday*, and *Edify*. Killackey is a contributing writer for The Young Catholic Woman website and its magazine, *Vigil*.

She lives with her family in the Tampa, Florida, area.

www.magdalaministries.org
YouTube: https://www.youtube.com/channel/UCnfTbi6mnXa8c Po8vehtTwA
Podcast: https://www.magdalaministries.org/podcast